hot california graphics
2

hot california graphics

2

MADISON SQUARE PRESS / NEW YORK

Madison Square Press
10 East 23rd Street
New York, NY 10010
Phone (864) 885-9444
Fax (864) 885-1090

Distributors to the trade in the United States and Canada:
BHB
108 East North First Street
Seneca, SC 29678

Distributors outside the United States and Canada:
HarperCollins International
10 East 53rd Street
New York, NY 10022-5299

Library of Congress Cataloging in Publication Data:
Entertainment Destinations

Printed in Hong Kong
ISBN 0-942604-48-2

Jacket Design: Hunt Design Associates

CONTENTS

INTRODUCTION

Thought music has often been described as the universal language; one glance at the pages of HOT CALIFORNIA GRAPHICS 2 will make you suspect graphic design has attained the same status. The brands, products and other visual representations of leading businesses and institutions are becoming increasingly recognizable around the world, and much of the credit goes to graphic design.

Providers of goods and services are increasingly turning to graphic design to create powerful visual tools for establishing and building unique identities that can attract and retain customers. What they have discovered is that the ability to escape anonymity and embrace a desirable corporate persona has become virtually mandatory in an ever more crowded marketplace. Far from being an abstract idea, graphic design helps them market and sell products in every specific way. Organizations that wish to position or reposition themselves in the market, define differences between themselves and competitors, signal internal changes to the outside world, attract attention for whatever reason, or trigger specific intellectual and emotional responses, can turn to graphic design for help.

One of the reasons graphic design can do this, of course, is that it is being applied more intensively than ever before. Just as any language has unlimited use when it is spoken by a growing number of speakers, graphic design is a visual language that attains astonishing utility when consumers can see it on as many visible aspects of life as possible. Just look at how effectively a business selling an express delivery service such as Federal Express, has harnessed the power of graphic design to give its business forms, Web site, retail stores, aircraft, packaging, trucks, signs, delivery workers' uniforms and advertising an unmistakable character that people recognize instantly from Market Street in San Francisco to Park Avenue in New York — and countless places overseas.

The ascendance of graphic design is the spread of international art commerce, which depends on visible symbols that are easy to comprehend no matter what spoken language or cultural norms prevail wherever multinational corporations collide in their quest for market share. Graphic Design has evolved into a highly condensed form of communication that can deliver its message at the speed of light when that's all the time it has.

Editors

maddocks & company
2011 pontius avenue
los angeles california 90025
310.477.4227
www.maddocks.com

maddocks & company

Maddocks & Company simply maintains that good work stems from a profound effort to understand the client's need, criteria and objectives. Anchored by Frank Maddocks, the company has created successful programs for such recognizable clients as Ketel One, Red Bull, Disney, Procter & Gamble, Sony, and Warner Bros. Rather than focus on developing its own look, Maddocks has built distinct, and powerful brand identities, product, packaging and merchandising programs that reflect highly conceptual and creative solutions tailored to each client's goals and objectives, establishing a clear connection between smart strategies and long-term success.

Ketel One. Clean, consistent design, and a new infusion of color have given this brand a strong retail presence and a competitive edge despite growing competition and no consumer advertising.

1

2

3

4

5

6

7

8

9

1. Ketel One gift packaging
2. Ketel One summer drink on-premise tent card
3. Ketel One Martini Madness on-premise tent card
4. Ketel One Apple Martini on-premise tent card
5. Ketel One introduction of Citroen
6. Ketel One summer drink on-premises bin and header
7/8. Ketel One website
9. Ketel One millennium gift box

PlayStation

1

2

3

HOME STYLE

THE VENETIAN

4

5

6

BOOKNET

gelson's cookware connection

CALIFORNIA FOOD & VENDING

7

8

9

girlCare

365 murad

CITY connection

10

11

12

Cutex

PHILIPS INTERACTIVE MEDIA

Axius

13

14

15

1

2

gelson's
cookware
connection

3

4

1. La Brea Bakery
2. Beefeater holiday packaging
3. El Cholo brand and packaging program
4/5. Gelson's brand and packaging program

5

13

1

2

3

1. Murad 365 brand and packaging program
2-5. Lunasol brand and packaging program

4

5

1

Sony Playstation. The powerful icon, Polygon Man, integrated into packaging, merchandising and in-store displays, launched the industry's hottest new gaming hardware and became the centerpiece for all advertising.

2

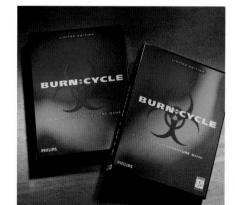

4

Disney. Bringing to life the beloved characters with original concepts, components and designs for over 120 SKUs, resulted in unprecedented top sellers.

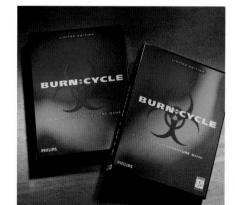

5

1. White Camellia brand and packaging program
2. Disney
3. Disney bath product and packaging design
4. Sony Playstation packaging design
5. Phillips packaging design

3

1

2

3

4

5

6

7

8

9

1. Platinum Equity logo identity
2/3. The Venetian logo identity and print program
4. Platinum Equity print program
5-7. The Fashion Institute of Design & Merchandising website
8. Platinum Equity website
9. Playboy Latin America website

370 South Doheny Drive, No. 201
Beverly Hills, Califonia 90211

ADAMSMORIOKA

Confluence: 1. A flowing together of two or more streams. 2. A convergence of ideas.

Founded in 1993, AdamsMorioka quickly gained an international reputation for leading the movement of simple clear work in brand development. Adams Morioka's process has been called "Design CPR," based on the manifesto of "clarity, purity and resonance," and is the soul of confluence.

Their strategies, along with the accompanying content and visual systems, have reinvigorated some of the nation's largest corporate brands. Clients include The Walt Disney Company, the Gap, ABC, and Old Navy. AdamsMorioka works in a wide range of media — print, environmental, inter-active, online and broadcast. Recently, Adams Morioka has been at the center of several television networks' redesign and strategic repositioning, including VH-1, Nickelodeon, Nick At Nite and TNN.

Unique among communications consultancies, AdamsMorioka not only plans and implements brand management programs, but also forms complete visual solutions and systems. These solutions powerfully engage the clients' audience and deliver larger strategic messages effortlessly. There are no restraints to ideas, no arbitrary design decisions in AdamsMorioka's work, just clear and honest communications that resonate emotionally and intellectually. That's why AdamsMorioka's images work— they are both seductive and accessible, refined to the most essential and direct.

AdamsMorioka has been recognized with numerous awards and exhibitions, including a solo exhibition at the San Francisco Museum of Modern Art. Their primary achievements, however, remain their contributions to the success of their clients.

1.

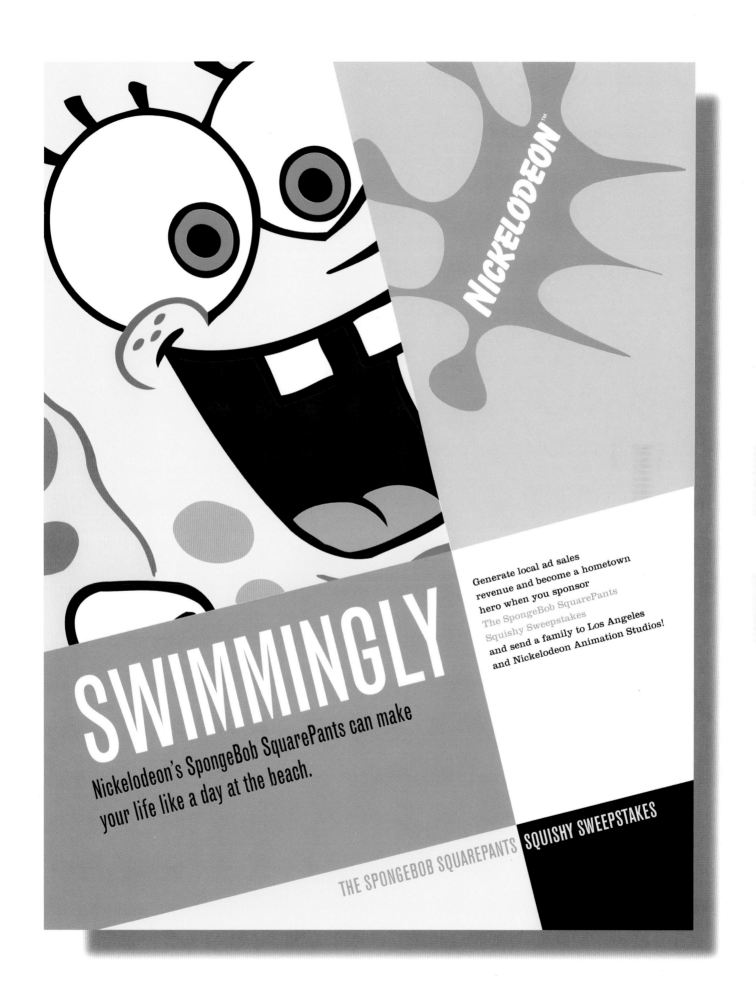

SWIMMINGLY

Nickelodeon's SpongeBob SquarePants can make your life like a day at the beach.

NICKELODEON™

Generate local ad sales revenue and become a hometown hero when you sponsor The SpongeBob SquarePants Squishy Sweepstakes and send a family to Los Angeles and Nickelodeon Animation Studios!

THE SPONGEBOB SQUAREPANTS SQUISHY SWEEPSTAKES

1.

1. Film Festival id and poster
2. Film production company
3. Architecture school
4. Talent agency
5. 2001 AIGA National Conference
6. Theme restaurant at LAX
7. Television network
8. Hair care products
9. Themed environment
10. On-line music company
11. Themed environment
12. Restaurant and martini bar
13. On-line music corporation
14. Paper company promotion
15. On-line directory service
16. Priceline.com
17. Television network

Bob Industries

2.

3.

ARTISTS MANAGEMENT GROUP

4.

5.

6.

The National Network

7.

8.

9.

10.

11.

12.

13.

14.

15.

16.

17.

AdamsMorioka

1.

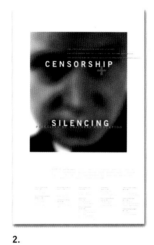

2.

3.

4.

5.

6.

7.

8.

9.

1.

2.

1.   Nick at Nite reface
2.   ESPN Winter X Games commercials
     Weiden and Kennedy: agency
     Dayton Faris: directors

Hunt Design Associates
25 North Mentor Ave
Pasadena, CA 91106
626.793.7847
fax 626.793.2549
huntdesign.com

HUNT DESIGN ASSOCIATES

Housed in their own historic brick building in the culturally aware city of Pasadena, Hunt Design Associates is a leading firm in the ever-evolving design field of Environmental Graphics. "We focus on graphic design for buildings, places and spaces," says principal Wayne Hunt. Hunt Design combines the classic principles of two-dimensional graphic design with processes and techniques of architecture and industrial design.

The firm is comprised of designers, drafts persons and programmers. Each has an interest in the built environment — how places are designed and constructed, and how people interact with physical space. "We pride ourselves in being active participants in the real world, not the virtual world," states Hunt, a veteran of thirty years in design — he started Hunt Design in 1977 after a few critical years in a well-known Los Angeles design firm.

Hunt Design has built an enviable reputation in the exciting people-based fields of transportation, entertainment, retail, and hospitality, executing major projects for the Walt Disney Company, MGM Grand, Universal, Warner Bros., and Park Place Entertainment. In addition, the firm extends its reach to exhibition design and visitor destinations of all kinds, including Kennedy Space Center, The New Jersey Aquarium and Chicago's Sears Tower. "We like to work on and be part of the places people want to go to learn and have fun while creating a sense of community," concludes Hunt.

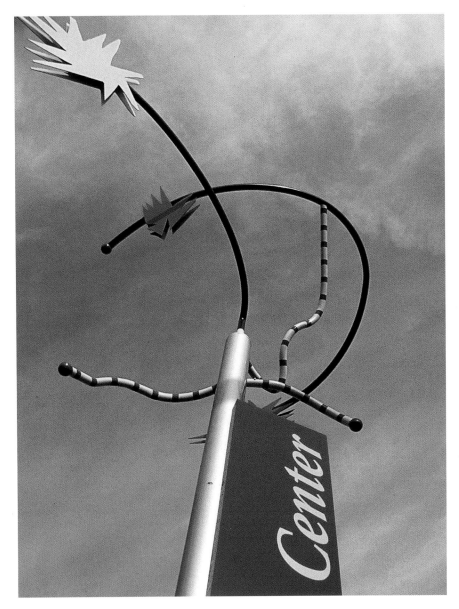

Downtown Wichita | Wichita, KS

A unique wayfinding and signage program helps revitalize the downtown core of Wichita.

FASHION DISTRICT

Bunker Hill →

BUNKER HILL

↑ Little Tokyo

↑ Civic Center

Disney Hall
Music Center →

HISTORIC DOWNTOWN

← Historic Broadway

→ Spring St Historical

↑ Grand Central Market

↑ Biddy Mason Park

↑ Ronald Reagan Bldg

↑ Library Tower

FIGUEROA CORRIDOR

→ USC

↑ Calif Afro-Amer Mus

↑ Calif Science Ctr

↑ Exposition Park

↑ Natural History Mus

← Metro Rail Ⓜ

Downtown Los Angeles Walks

Thirteen downtown districts are unified in a comprehensive 300 block wayfinding program.

with Corbin

27

Chicano Now!

A bold series of graphic panels captures the rich
history and contributions of Chicanos in America.

for Clear Channel Entertainment-Exhibitions; with Wyatt Design

Sears Tower Skydeck | Chicago

The many stories of Chicago are told in a dynamic graphic display on the 103rd floor.

with Delmont Liesure

Rose Bowl | Pasadena, CA

A comprehensive signage program
for the hundred-year-old stadium,
adjacent parking and pedestrian areas.

Urban Gateways define downtown
areas for Oxnard, Brea and Inglewood.

James Robie Design Associates
152 1/2 N. La Brea Avenue
Los Angeles, California 90036-2912
323.939.7370
jrobie@robie.com
www.robie.com

JAMES ROBIE DESIGN ASSOCIATES

For the past 23 years James Robie Design Associates has built a reputation for effective award-winning work, integrity, and sound designer-client relationships. These long-term client relationships are the result of communication solutions and streamlined project coordination that produce projects that are truly successful.

Hype is not our style. Simplicity, unpretentiousness, and honesty are more like it, both in our design and our interactions with our clients.

We produce design driven by effectiveness – not by the latest trend, or what the newest advance in technology allows us to do, or by a signature style regardless of whether it's appropriate. Our work is grounded in classic principles of design, emphasizing clarity, which is the result of proper fusion between form and content.

We are dedicated to the pursuit of good graphic design and our staff works very hard to make it look very easy.

The events of September 11, 2001 have changed the world as we know it forever. 9/11/01 and the events that are occurring as I write this make one thing very clear: America and western civilization are fighting for the very right to be free.

As a designer, the very essence of my profession is freedom. It is freedom to create, freedom to compete, freedom to judge, freedom to offend and even the freedom to fail. I know we will be able to continue to design and create only as long as we are successful in defeating those who would like to destroy the society we have built.

Remember 9.11.01

1

2

1. Multi-media press kit
2. Corporate magazine for aerospace-technology company

SERVING YOUTH THROUGH SPORT

1

2

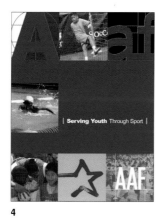

4

5

6

1. Identity for non-profit youth organization
2. Identity manual
3. Coaches flyer
4. Biennial report
5. Medal, hat, T-shirt
6. Newsletter

1

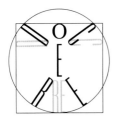

2

3

4

1. Marketing brochure for real estate company
2. Identity for media company
3. Annual report for executive recruitment firm
4. Marketing brochure for financial printer

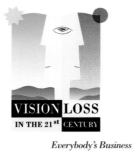

1

2

3

4

5

6

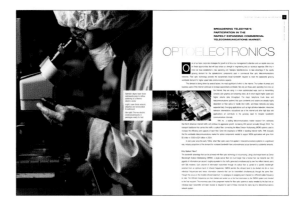

1. Identity for real estate company
2. Identity for vision loss conference
3. Identity for catering company
4. Identity manual for youth sports organization
5. Capital campaign for private school
6. Annual report for technology company

1

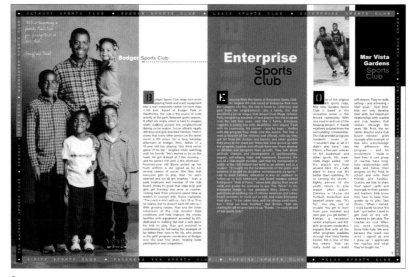

2

3

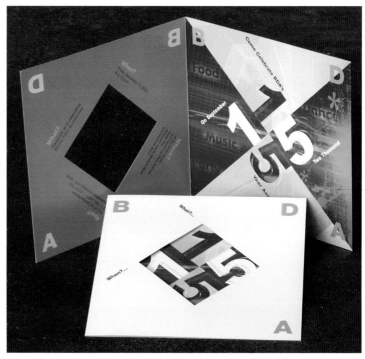

4

1. Direct mail piece for printing company
2. Report for non-profit youth organization
3. Identity for bakery
4. Invitation for interior designer

1

2

3

4

5

1. Marketing materials for architect
2. Announcement for ancient art museum
   lecture series
3. Annual reports for financial company
4. Annual report for private school
5. Logo for children's camp anniversary

1

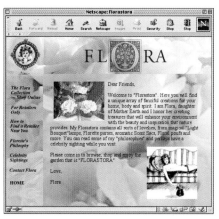

2

1. Identity and web site for multi-media company
2. Identity and web site for floral gift company

Sackett Design Associates
2103 Scott Street
San Francisco, CA 94115-2120
Voice: 415.929.4800
Fax: 415.929.4819
www.sackettdesign.com
E-mail: info@sackettdesign.com

SACKETT DESIGN ASSOCIATES

Founded in 1988, Sackett Design Associates has become a highly regarded, award-winning design, branding, multimedia product development, and marketing communications company. Headquartered in San Francisco, with a second office in Los Angeles, Sackett Design has a staff of nine print, retail and multimedia designers, directors, and account management personnel. The firm of San Francisco occupies two buildings in the Pacific Heights neighborhood; which house the company's principle operations, as well as its subsidiaries: Circa Props, antique prop rentals (with its thousands of antique toys, game boards, dolls, packaging, and advertising items); Republic of Sound, the firm's recording label; and Stage 24 Productions, its event production division.

Mark Sackett, principal owner and creative director, and his staff have won over 850 industry awards in national and international design competitions. Their work has been published in numerous design annuals, books, and competitions including The AIGA Communications Graphics Show,

Communication Arts, Graphis, American Corporate Identity, California Graphic Design, San Francisco Design, How Magazine, Step-by-Step Graphics, Hot California Graphics and Print. Additionally, their work is included in the permanent collection of the Library of Congress.

Sackett Design Associates continually selects assignments where they can collaborate with their clients in the creation of strategic dynamic solutions and integrated brand development. In addition, they have designed and implemented a corporate creativity training program entitled Brainfood Creative Programs,™ for corporations with in-house marketing and creative departments. Brainfood focuses primarily on team building, trends analysis, cognitive skills development, research techniques, and motivational programs, designed to improve individual and team productivity as well as their creative results. Mark Sackett also speaks around the country at conferences and seminars about their Brainfood programs and the firm's work.

1. Pocket folder for Warner Bros. Studio Stores International Advertising. (Generic template print ads for Warner Bros. Studio Stores International Advertising **2–4**)

5. Corporate identity and business papers for Cliffside Entertainment, an independent recording studio and film production company. (Identity and business papers **6–7**)

1

2

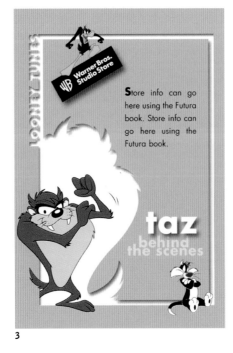

3

4

5

6

7

1

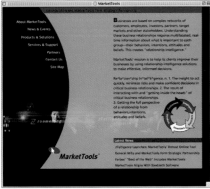

2

1. Media Kit for MarketTools, an online market research company.
2. Website for MarketTools.
3. Identity for Everychild Foundation, a non-profit organization located in Los Angeles, CA.
4. Trade print ads for DiCon Fiberoptics (Subsequent print ads **5–6**)
7. Business papers for MarketTools.
8. Product brochure for MarketTools and their zTelligence product.

EVERYCHILD
FOUNDATION

3

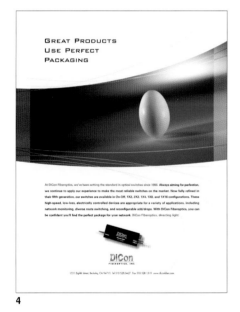

GREAT PRODUCTS
USE PERFECT
PACKAGING

4

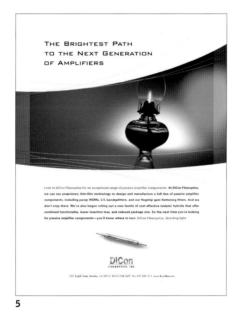

THE BRIGHTEST PATH
TO THE NEXT GENERATION
OF AMPLIFIERS

5

ONE GOOD TECHNOLOGY
SERVING ANOTHER

6

7

8

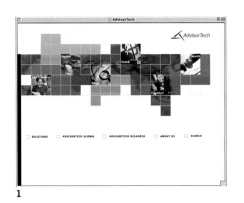
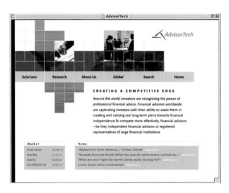
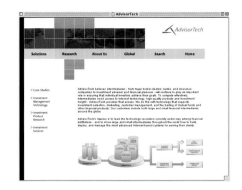

1

2

3

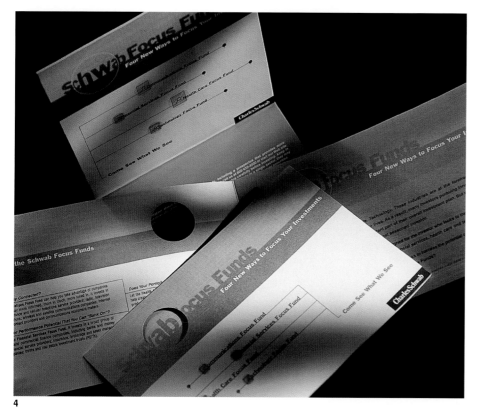

4

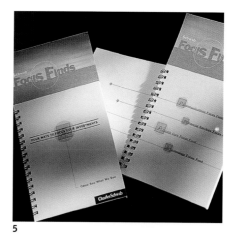

5

6

7

1. Website for AdvisorTech, an independent financial consulting firm.

2. Press kit for AdvisorTech.

3. Coasters and invitation for Sackett Design Associates' Bowl-A-Rama holiday party.

4. Retail in-branch display and direct mail for Charles Schwab & Co., Inc., Schwab Focus Funds launch.

5. Lead kit for Charles Schwab & Co., Inc., Schwab Focus Funds launch. (Subsequent spreads **6–7**)

2

1

3

1. Corporate identity for WorkPlace Answers, a company offering web-based harassment prevention classes for U.S. based corporations.

2. Retail in-branch display and direct mail for Charles Schwab & Co., Inc., Bond Funds launch.

3. Annual report for Power Integrations, a leading computer chip manufacturer. (Interior Spreads **4–5**)

4

5

1337 Third Street Promenade
Santa Monica, CA 90401
Tel 310.576.1070
Fax 310.576.1074
www.sargentberman.com

SARGENT & BERMAN, INC.

Sargent & Berman helps its clients achieve their creative and financial goals through sensible, innovative solutions driven by strategic and creative expertise.

Over the past 15 years, they've worked with high-profile companies in industries as diverse as technology & telecommunications, toys, travel & tourism, health care, fashion, food and beverage, and entertainment. And, over 70% of their business comes from clients they've worked with for over 10 years. S&B attributes this kind of loyalty to their results-focused design philosophy:

Outstanding creative executions not based on focused marketing strategies are ineffective, while sound strategic thinking will always break through the marketing clutter if given powerful creative expression.

S&B approaches every project as a unique event that must fit within the context of a company's overall marketing plan and goals. The following examples of their recent work demonstrate S&B's design philosophy in action.

2

3

4

1. Princess Cruises Destination Brochure
2. Princess Cruises Passenger Ticket Organizer
3. Princess Cruises Travel Agent Promotion
4. Princess Cruises Onboard Theatrical Posters

1

2

> CORPORATE IDENTITY

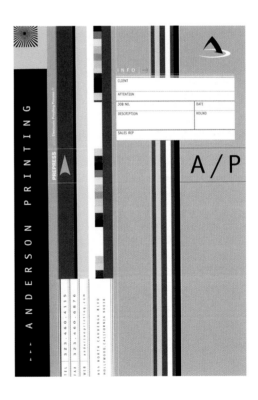

1. Anderson Printing Corporate Logo
2. Anderson Printing Identity System
3. Anderson Printing Job Folders

3

1

2

3

1. EspriTV Sales Brochure
2. EspriTV Corporate Logo
3. EspriTV Identity System

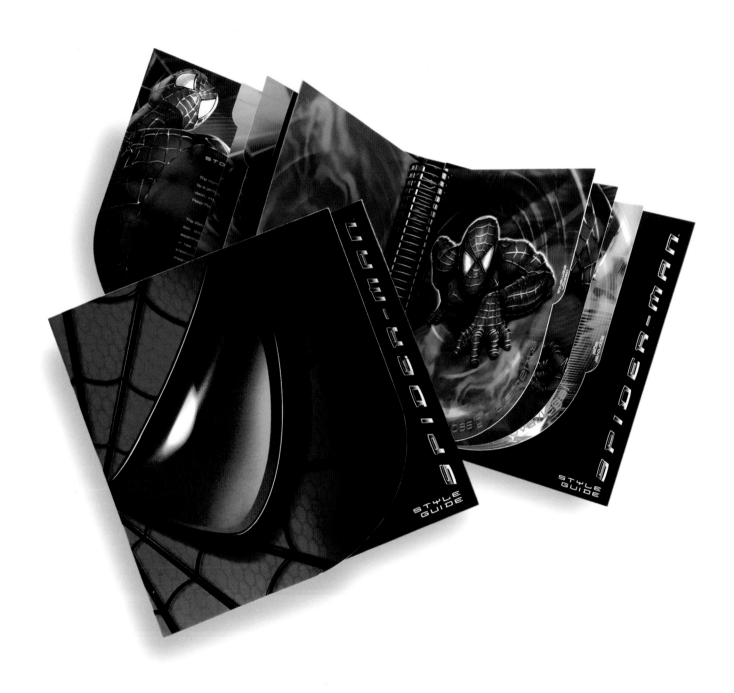

2

3

4

1. Sony Pictures Consumer Products
Spider-Man Style Guide

2. Sony Pictures Consumer Products
Charlie's Angel's Style Guide

3. Sony Pictures Consumer Products
Max Steel Style Guide

4. Bond Marketing 007 Style Guide

1

2

> PRODUCT PACKAGING

1. Bandai America Extreme DX Finger Boards
2. Jakks Pacific WWF WrestleMania 3D
3. Hansen's Natural Soy Juice Smoothie

3

Evenson Design Group
4445 Overland Avenue
Culver City, California 90230
Tel: 310.204.1995
Fax: 310.204.4879
www.evensondesign.com

EVENSON DESIGN GROUP

Collector's Item: An object worth placing in a collection because of its beauty, value, or interest.

Most of EDG's clients have the opportunity to visit our office and are instantly surrounded by a vast exhibit of vintage signage, antique metal toy trucks, 1920's and '30's trophies and folk art made from recycled artifacts. It's Stan Evenson's second passion that gives the EDG studio an inviting, amusing, and eclectic personality that instantly tames even the most frenzied spirit. And no one can resist the jovial effects of the life-sized framed photograph of Roy Rogers (Trigger had already passed on) that greets every guest with a smile as they enter our office.

Stan's first passion, however, is to bring the beauty, value and the interest of others to each and every one of EDG's projects by submerging himself and his team of designers into their client's brand. Though the ultimate solution is likely to not be retro driven, it's the strategic planning that allows EDG to provide an effective extension of their client's marketing goals for the present and the future.

With over 25 years of experience and expertise in the design field,

EDG is one of the oldest and most respected design firms in the US. "We've successfully endured through the hardest of times, against recessions and budding design competitors since our start up in 1976", reflects Stan. "EDG's clients consistently come back to the table again and again because they receive more than great design that delivers results. They also get hands on service that makes every client feel that they're the only one. I'm the first to admit that the competition is fierce out there as I witnessed when judging a recent Communication Arts design competition with over 15,000 entries. I'm pleased to say that my design firm has the integrity and the staying power that our clients deserve and have come to expect."

Today, EDG serves clients as far away as China and as close as our next-door neighbor. It's the global economy and worldwide branding that EDG transcends with a real human touch. If staying in front of your competition and having the crowd focus on your brand above the rest is important to you, then let EDG bring a magnitude of beauty, value, and interest to your company, service, or product. We invite you to visit our gallery of fine collectibles at www.evensondesign.com.

1. **EDG Clocks** This holiday promotion for our clients and friends celebrated the New Millennium with eight different clock faces telling the story of our timeless design and timely creative process.

2. **Stan's Holiday Rub** A special blend helping clients and friends spice up the holidays became our 2000-2001 "Seasoned Greetings" holiday message.

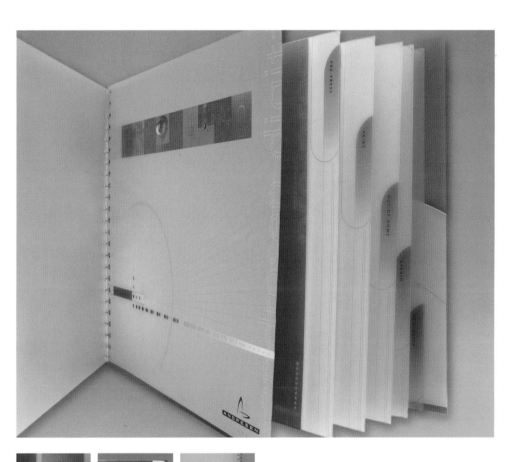

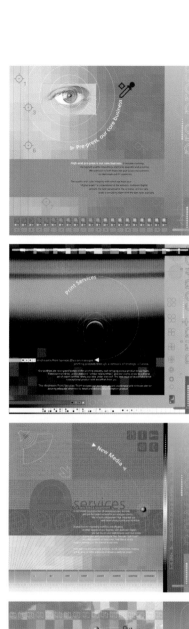

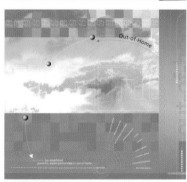

Andresen Capabilities Brochure Creating out-of-this world imagery, EDG captured the essence of Andresen Digital Prepress' state-of-the-art service and capabilities through this full-color brochure that allows constant updates as new technologies emerge.

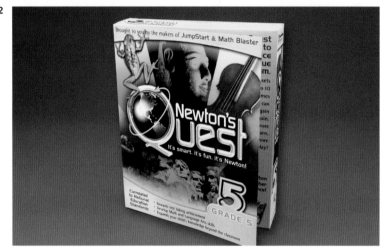

1. Math & Reading Blaster Dynamic packaging and logo design was created for this complete line of interactive and educational software for kids 4th-6th grades.

2. Newton's Quest Creating excitement for learning, EDG designed this colorful packaging and logo for this advanced educational software for kids 4th-6th grades.

3. Communicate & Connect EDG provided this contemporary and sophisticated redesign of the packaging and logo for this line of language-aid software from Berlitz.

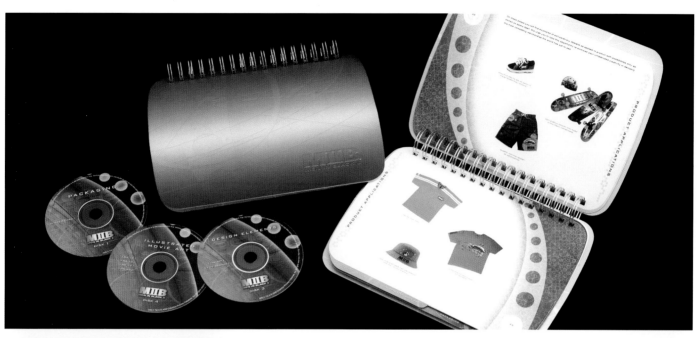

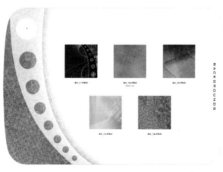
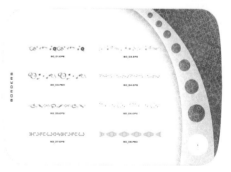

MIB II Style Guide This 10-CD, 46-page style guide showcases art and ideas for potential trade manufacturers. Everything from each page to all artwork was created by a team of designers and illustrators with the MIB II movie theme in mind. From top photo to bottom: style guide, sample pages, tab designs, logos.

EN⊙PHERICS

Enspherics Corporate ID System A high-tech, digital security company was in need of a new logo and identity to hit high-profile clients. Starting from the logo, a complete stationery system including, mailing labels, custom printed CD Roms, CD case sleeves, and floppy disk labels were designed. Additional marketing pieces such as a press kit folder, brochure, ads, and trade show booth display were also created to complete this identity. From top photo to bottom: logo, stationery, reception area signage, trade booth display, brochure.

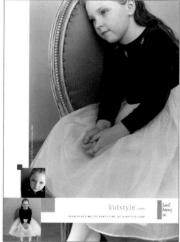

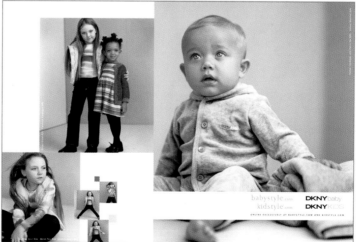

1. Consumer Ads for estyle.com featured in Martha Stewart Baby A series of 11 spreads and 17 single-page ads were created for estyle.com, babystyle.com and kidstyle.com to present their fall collection. *Note: the cover was not designed by EDG.

2. Kidstyle.com Launch Party Invitation A unique and fun invitation celebrating the launch of kidstyle.com.

Acura Music Festival
NFL New England Patriots
Angel City Fitness: gym

St. Vincent Medical Center:
  proposed logo
DoubleGreen: landscape design
Resolution Economics: litigation
  and economics consulting group

The Giving Tree: fundraising
  & public relations
Brooks Howard: consulting
Colorado Space Business
  Roundtable

La Carte aux Trésors: proposed logo
  for a reality show in France
ERAS Center: educational center for
  "at risk" children
Moveline: relocation services

Idyllwild Jazz in the Pines Festival
Little League World Series
Cubby's Coffee House

Laura Coe Design Associates
4918 North Harbor Drive, Ste. 206
San Diego, California 92106
619.223.0909
Fax 619.223.0939
lcw@coedesign.com
www.coedesign.com

LAURA COE DESIGN ASSOCIATES

Laura Coe Design Associates has earned
a national reputation as a leader in brand
identity, packaging and retail environments.
Created in 1985, by owner Laura Coe
Wright, LCDA places special emphasis on
the marketing integration of two- and
three-dimensional images.

Highly experienced, with a broad range of
clients, their work is strategic, focused and
conceptually driven. While the projects are
varied, a sound strategy along with creative
excellence is consistently the key to success.

Collaboration is also an important aspect
of their work. Whether it be with the client,
the photographer or the fabricator, Laura
is quick to credit her staff for operating
creatively, intelligently and efficiently.

Simply put, LCDA creates exceptional visual
design solutions that cause memorable
impressions and generates results.

1

2

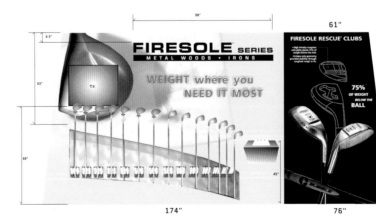

3

Branding Series for Taylor Made Golf

1. Softgoods Environment
2. Interactive Kiosks and Concept Drawings
   for PGA Trade Show
3. Putter Display with Information Booklet
4. Product Introduction Sales Kit
5. Branding for Corporate Communications
6. Special Product Promotional Kit

4

5

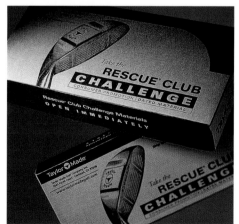

6

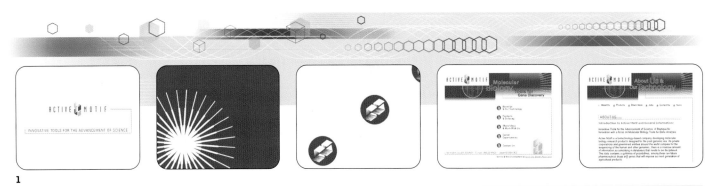

1

2

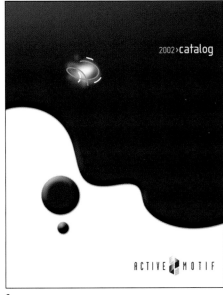

3

Branding Series for Active Motif

1. Internet Brand Design and Development
2. Brand Development for Corporate Identity
3. Product Catalog
4. Packaging System for Products

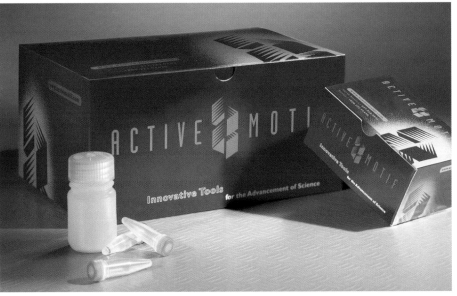

4

1

2

3

4

5

1. Promotional Logo - Mitsubishi
2. "Big Fish and Small Fish" - Self Promotion Illustration
3. Direct Mail Promotion - Zoological Society of San Diego
4. "Gorilla in Love" - Self Promotion Illustration
5. Hotel Lobby Display - SeaWorld of California

1. "Young Creator" - Self Promotion Illustration
2. Brand Packaging for Nutritional Products -
   As We Change
3. Consumer Product Packaging -
   Hewlett-Packard Company
4. Brand Packaging for Hair Care Products -
   As We Change

1

3

Branding Series for Printing Industries Association

1. Brand Development for Identity

2. Event Communication System

3. Environmental Banners

4. Trade Show Collateral

2

4

1

5

9

2

MOTIVA

6

10

3

7

BALLENA
VISTA
FARM

11

4

PrimaVu

8

12

1. Proposed Census Icon
2. Breathable Fabric Icon
3. Calendar Editorial Icon
4. Proposed Census Icon

5. Outdoor Lighting Company Identity
6. Software Company Identity
7. Theatrical Play Logo
8. Eye Care Product Identity

9. Customer Service Icon
10. On-Line Connectivity Icon
11. Thoroughbred Farm Identity
12. Permeable Fabric Icon

835 Fifth Avenue
San Rafael, CA 94901
415.485.5760

www.cymbic.com

CYMBIC

cymbic™

Cymbic is a marketing communications firm with a worldwide reputation for positioning, branding, and marketing high-tech businesses and products.

With considerable experience in some of the most competitive markets, Cymbic has helped more than 150 companies build and extend their brands from startup to IPO with traditional and technology-based marketing initiatives.

Cymbic's unique methodology blends creative discipline, positioning strategy, and technical savvy to combine the best skills typically found separately among PR, marketing, design and Web firms. This integrated approach helps clients cut through clutter with sustainable and scalable brands that achieve measurable business results.

Cymbic believes that a brand represents the relationship between your business and your stakeholders. The relationship may be symbolized by your logo, look or voice, but the roots reach deeply into day-to-day interactions. Those interactions are the front line of your brand—the critical link in connecting marketing strategies with business results.

All interactions happen through Touchpoints—the assets through which you communicate with your audience. As a group, your Touchpoints form a system that is your corporate fingerprint—the distinct impression you leave behind on everything you touch.

Cymbic's proprietary method for solving marketing challenges focuses on the unique system of Touchpoints that defines each business. Because Touchpoints are tangible, Cymbic's approach ensures measurable results, clear marketing strategies, and consistent communications.

As new technologies emerge, the complexity and scope of Touchpoints increases dramatically. In order to succeed, businesses need to close the gap between their traditional marketing and new technology initiatives, and Cymbic has structured its business to help clients take this critical step.

Above picture: *Principals left to right,* Russ Baker, Chris Kenton, Kenichi Nishiwaki

1

Iospan Wireless provides a revolutionary system of broadband wireless access products. Cymbic developed a complete marketing communications system for Iospan, designed to personify the freedom and power embodied in wireless telecommunications.

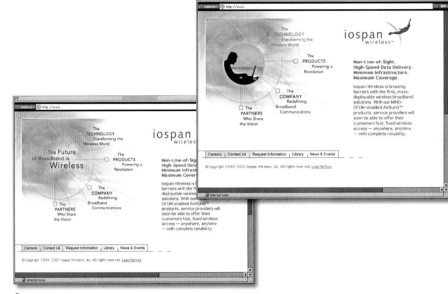

2

3

4

5

1. Corporate Identity
2. Web site
3. Flash Identity Intro
4. Product Brochure
5. Presentation Folder

Securify provides sophisticated security products and services for Fortune 2000 businesses. Securify engaged Cymbic to overhaul the strategic direction and design of their entire marketing communications program to build a consistent brand message.

1. Corporate and Product Brochures
2. Web site
3. Presentation Folder

1

Sendmail, Inc. delivers the Internet's mail–literally. Sendmail's Mail Transfer Agent software is responsible for routing and delivering as much as 85% of all email. Built on the foundation of an Open Source community, Sendmail was incorporated in 1997 to market a commercial version of its software. Cymbic has worked with Sendmail from the start to build and continually evolve a complex brand image that is at once highly technical and community-oriented.

2

3

4

1. Corporate Identity

2. Web site

3. Presentation Folder

4. Product Brochures

5. Product Online Demo

6. Product Packaging

7. Online Identity Standards

8. Product CD and Cover

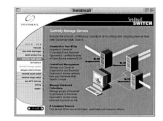

5

6

7

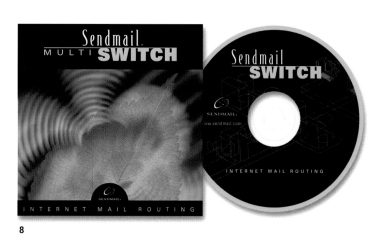

8

UTStarcom is a publicly traded telecommunications firm with an international presence. Cymbic created a complete marketing communications system to support UTStarcom's image as a global provider of cutting edge products.

1. UTStarcom Corporate Brochure
2. UTStarcom Product Brochure
3. CD Business Card

Cymbic created a fast and lean Web site for networking provider P-Cube, focusing on international accessibility and engineering sensibilities.

4. Web site

1

Cable giant Charter Communications tapped Cymbic to extend the Charter brand online with an eCommerce site to attract and convert retail cable subscribers.

1. Web site

2

Cymbic created the shopping experience for Americas largest wholesale marketplace, AmericasMart.

2. Web site

3

Motorola asked Cymbic to create the concept and interface for an Internet/TV crossover site, combining the strengths of video-on-demand, eCommerce, and real-time television programming.

3. Proof-of-concept Web site

79

1

2

3

4

5

6

1. Quantum Shift
2. Cyntric
3. Netro
4. Hyoshin (Hyogo Shinkin Bank)
5. KickFire
6. Kinecta

Mires
2345 Kettner Boulevard
San Diego, CA 92101
ph. 619.234.6631
fx. 619.234.1807
www.miresbrands.com

MIRES

Founded over 15 years ago, Mires has steadily grown to become a premier provider of brand-focused design and strategy to dedicated, driven market innovators.

Through the inspired application of brand principles to visual and non-visual communications, we add value to products and services and create preference in the marketplace. Our processes and solutions provide intensely competitive companies with practical insight, diligent follow-through, and impeccable execution.

At Mires, designers and marketing experts from wide-ranging backgrounds work in unified teams to develop the tools companies use to connect with their audiences. Accessibility and involvement, experience and experimentation, direction and dialog are all equally a part of each team solution.

By working outwards from a company's business objectives, and by keeping the context of the marketplace in constant view, Mires develops highly consistent messages and visually engaging solutions for programs of every level of depth and complexity. Additionally, by collaborating with clients at the highest levels of business and marketing strategy, Mires establishes the trust and executional blueprint that allow companies to reach consensus readily, make decisions quickly, and consider creative alternatives from the most informed perspective.

1

2

3

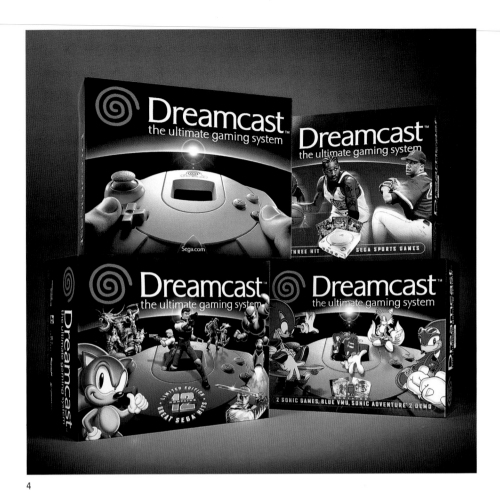

4

5

6

7

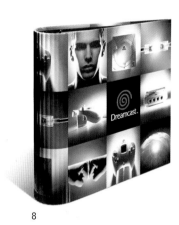

8

Visual branding for Sega® Dreamcast™ products

1. Online service identity
2. Point-of-purchase promotion
3. Product icon
4. Game system packaging
5. Poster
6. Tradeshow graphics
7. Tradeshow graphics
8. Sales collateral

1

2

3

4

5

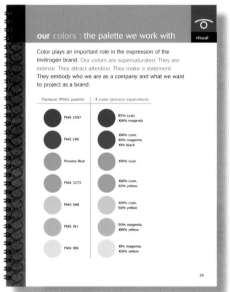

6

7

8

9

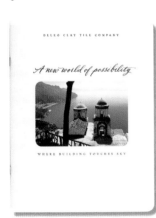

10

11

Visual branding for Taylor Guitars®

1. Dealer price lists
2. Point-of-purchase hangtag
3. Branded apparel catalog
4. Website
5. Product catalog

Visual branding for Arena Stage

6-8. Season brochure
9-10. Website

1

2

3

4

5

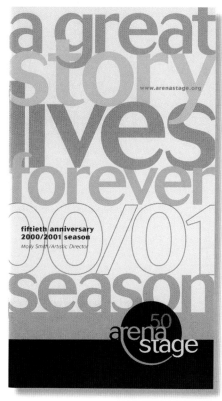

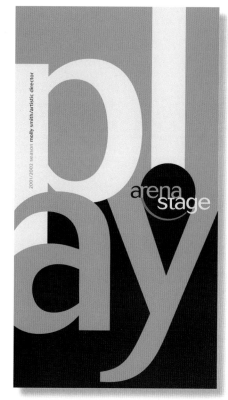

6

7

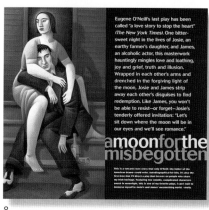

8

9

10

1

2

3

4

5

6

7

8

1. Tourism identity
2. Internet identity
3. Apparel/accessories identity
4. Computer game packaging
5. Sporting goods packaging
6. Sporting goods packaging
7. Telecommunications packaging
8. Automotive packaging

30sixty design, inc.
2801 Cahuenga Blvd. West
Los Angeles, California 90068
323.850.5311
info@30sixtydesign.com
www.30sixtydesign.com

30sixty design

For two decades, *30sixty design* has stepped outside the boundaries of the ordinary and the expected. With clients' resources, time constraints and market demands influencing all aspects of the creative process, *30sixty design* offers innovative solutions in creating strong, branded expressions. From consumer products to home entertainment to graphic design and product development, *30sixty design* has helped countless companies worldwide not only achieve their goals, but surpass them.

With an on-site staff of more than twenty professionals, whose diverse backgrounds include design, marketing, copywriting and interactive media development, *30sixty design* is well equipped to assemble capable design teams appropriate for any project. As the versatility and power of today's technology increases, *30sixty design* is committed to the unending exploration of new tools, techniques and media that allows them to remain at the forefront of advertising and design.

Harry Potter and The Sorcerer's Stone™ Illustrative Style Guide / Warner Bros. Consumer Products **1**
Harry Potter and The Sorcerer's Stone™ Illustrative Style Guide Supplement / Warner Bros. Consumer Products **2**
Harry Potter and The Sorcerer's Stone™ Theatrical Style Guide / Warner Bros. Consumer Products **3**

A   B   C   D

<table>
<tr><td colspan="3">4</td></tr>
<tr><td>5</td><td>6</td><td>7</td></tr>
</table>

4 Ferrari Youth Apparel Style Guide / Mattel®
5 The Scorpion King™ Style Guide / Universal Pictures
6 Star Trek® Digital Style Guide / Viacom Consumer Products
7 Josie™ and the Pussycats Style Guide / Universal Pictures

A-D Hot Wheels™ Style Guide Supplement Icons / Mattel®

<table>
<tr><td colspan="3">1</td></tr>
<tr><td>2</td><td>3</td><td>4</td></tr>
</table>

The Godfather® DVD Collection / Paramount Home Entertainment **1**
Real War / Simon & Schuster Interactive **2**
Bumper Wars / Simon & Schuster Interactive **3**
Pearl Harbor – Zero Hour / Simon & Schuster Interactive **4**

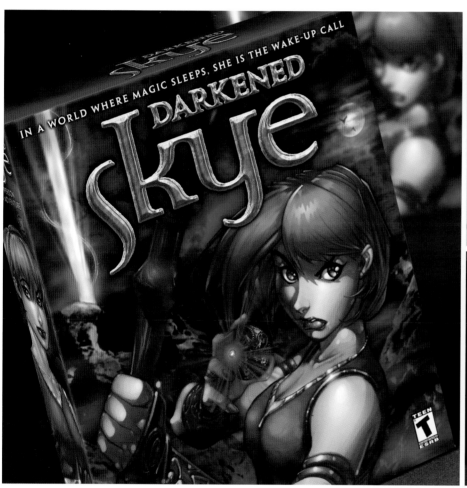

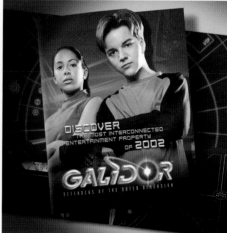

5 Darkened Skye / Simon & Schuster Interactive

6 The Conversation / Charlotte's Web / TITANIC – DVD Key Art and Packaging / Paramount Home Entertainment

7 GALIDOR™ Sell Sheet and Press Kit / CinéGroupe

PRODUCERS &
ENGINEERS WING

A   **B**   **C**   **D**

7 32° Degrees™ / Brewski Brewing Co.
8 Gorky's Beer / Gorky's Russian Brewery
9 Summer Tea / Williams-Sonoma, Inc.

Motown Records **A**
The National Academy of Recording Arts and Sciences® **B**
Rapax **C**
Remediation Resources **D**

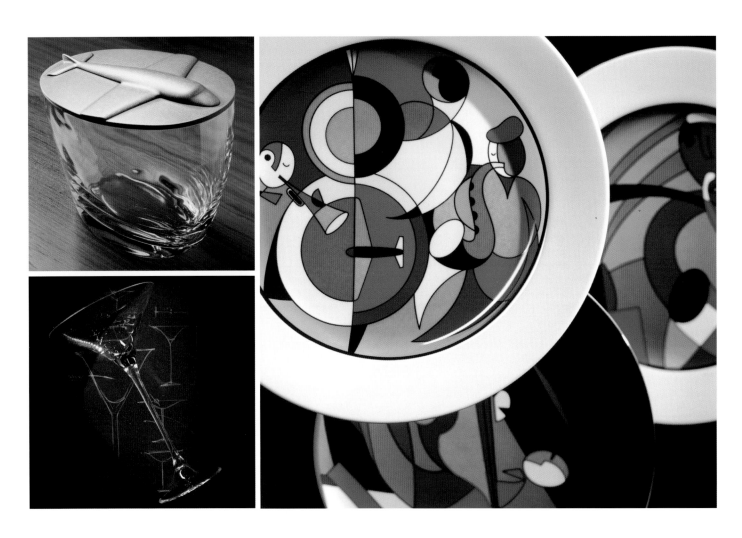

1
2
3

Aerobleu Ice Bucket / Less Than 7 **1**
Aerobleu Martini Glass / Less Than 7 **2**
Aerobleu China / Less Than 7 **3**

1411 Seventh Street
Santa Monica, California 90401

BAKER DESIGNED COMMUNICATIONS

Near the beach, in Santa Monica, California, Baker Designed Communications occupies a space that began as two different structures forming an old printing plant. When it came time to find a new office for his growing strategic design business, founder Gary Baker drew on his experience at problem solving and looked at the two old buildings from an entirely new perspective.

Focused on finding just the right combination of form and function, he designed a solution that effectively unifies the parts into an integrated, cohesive whole. That same philosophy drives the work that takes place inside Baker today. The Baker team uses strategy, creativity and execution to create "Designed Communications" that help clients succeed and grow.

1

VERACITY
CAPITAL PARTNERS

2

3

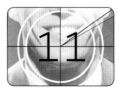

4

5

The firm is home to a group of talented strategists, writers and designers who bring a multi-disciplinary approach to bear. Their services include comprehensive branding and strategic consulting; integrated marketing communications; investor communications and interactive design services.

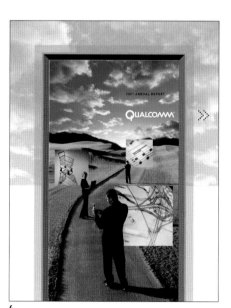

6

7

8

1. Sears Health & Nutrition Center poster
2. Veracity Capital Partners identity
3. Costello Brothers identity
4. November Films identity
5. Tenet identity
6. Qualcomm annual report
7. Baker annual self-promotion calendar
8. Dai-Ichi Kangyo Bank of California annual report

Baker works with a diverse client list including high profile brands like Adaptec, K2, Qualcomm, Tenet Healthcare, UCLA, Unocal and WellPoint. Impressive stories. Inspired strategy and design. Every client has a story to tell. And from annual reports and brand identities to marketing collateral and websites, Baker brings their stories to life.

1. Fluor magazine
2. WellPoint print and online annual report
3. Beckman Coulter print and online annual report
4. Best Foundation anti-drug poster
5. UCLA Capital Development video

4

alumni scholarships change
people's lives

alumni support gives
julia confidence

5

1

 guidance

2

3

 IndyMac Bank

4

The talented people at Baker have stories of their own. They are newlyweds, new moms, night students, morning folks, right-brainers, left-brainers. They're diverse, dynamic and dedicated. They work hard. And they get recognized for it by the usual suspects including the AIGA, AR 100, Communication Arts, Graphis and Print Design Annual, to name a few.

5

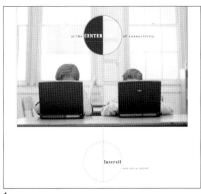

6

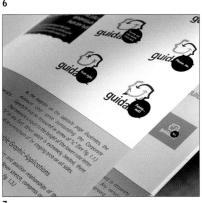

7

1. Guidance recruitment campaign

2. Guidance identity

3. Cobalt identity

4. IndyMac Bank identity

5. IndyMac Bank print and online annual report

6. Intersil annual report

7. Guidance graphic standards

Under the leadership of Gary Baker, they come together in teams — challenging and supportive throughout the creative process. They lend an ear, a hand and a voice to each other and to clients. Because ultimately, they all want the same thing: The best possible solution for the work at hand.

As Gary Baker says, "It all comes down to this: I want everyone to go home feeling proud of what they've done." That's the story at Baker Designed Communications. Putting the pieces together in a unique and compelling way. Just like the building they work in. Cohesive. On target. Different.

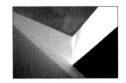

1

2

3

1. Ad Club of Los Angeles poster
2. MiniMed annual report
3. Mead/Xpedx promotion

1424 Marcelina Avenue
Torrance, CA 90501
Phone: 310.381.0170
Fax: 310.381.0169
Web: soohoodesign.com

SOOHOO DESIGNERS

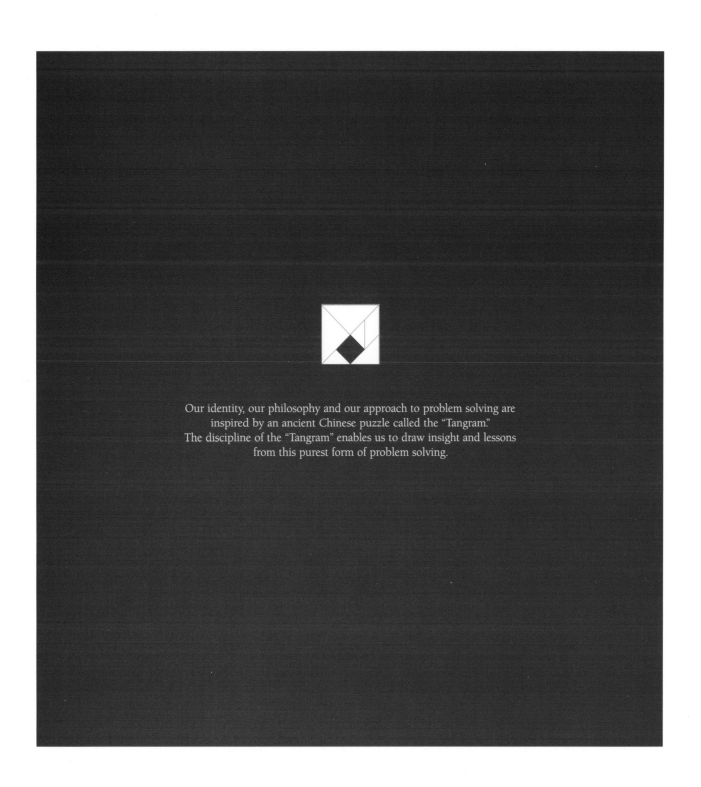

Our identity, our philosophy and our approach to problem solving are
inspired by an ancient Chinese puzzle called the "Tangram."
The discipline of the "Tangram" enables us to draw insight and lessons
from this purest form of problem solving.

Enlightened communication illuminates a pathway to more profitable business.

Bold strategic moves are the key to capturing additional market share.

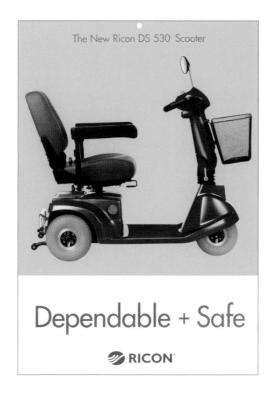

Only the truly gifted designer is able to produce quality in quantity.

Promotional and support materials
designed to generate interest for
Elar Partners' national sales meeting.

Relentless curiosity is a way to assure targeted communication.

1. Consumer travel brochures leveraging the Pleasant Holidays brand.

2. Rack brochure designed to promote the history, tradition and celebration of the Tournament of Roses Rose Parade and Rose Bowl Game.

3. Tournament of Roses chronological highlight poster.

1.

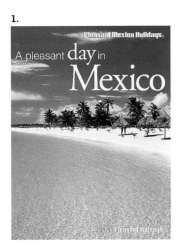

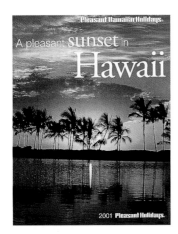

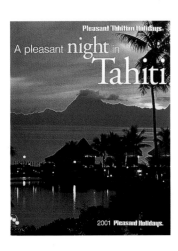

2.

3.

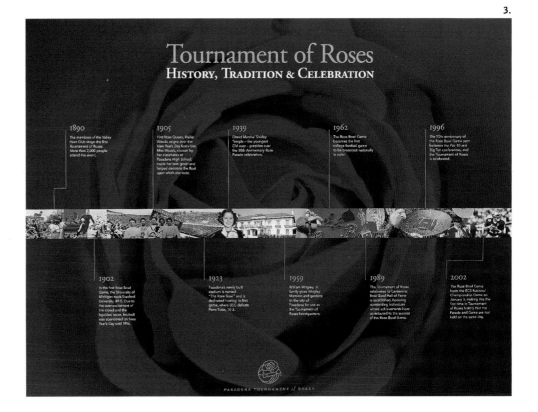

Joan D. Libera
Libera Design Inc.
Los Angeles, California 90064
San Francisco, California 94105
310.477.2027
415.777.2121
joan@liberadesign.com

Passion
Invention
Vision
Systems
Process
Intension
Reach
Explosive
Flexibility
Balance

LIBERA DESIGN INC.

Libera Design Inc. is a leading design
and marketing communications firm
providing a full spectrum of integrated,
value-added services targeted to the
corporate and financial communities.

We believe that quality, value and
responsiveness are critical factors
driving success for building business.

Libera Design Inc.

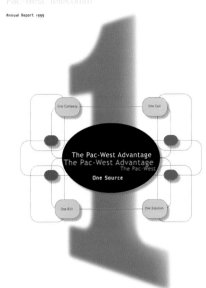

CLEARANT, INC.

QUBIC LIGHT

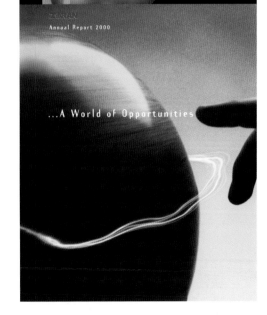

Passion
Invention
Vision

point 3 6 0

build 3 6 0

live 3 6 0

shock 3 6 0

digital 3 6 0

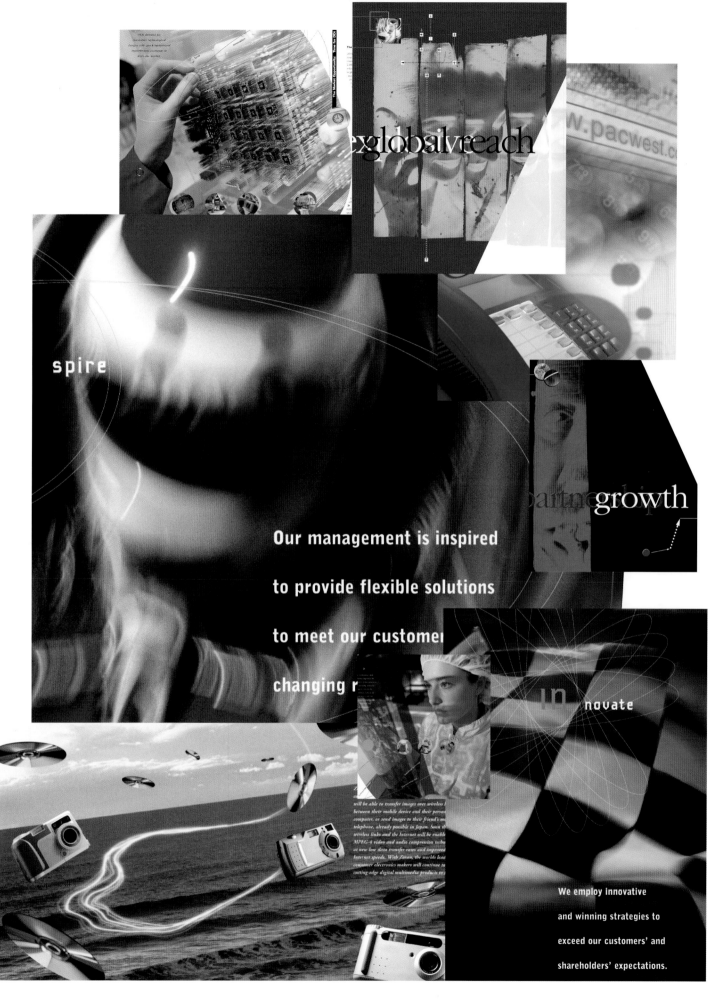

exglobalreach

w.pacwest.c

spire

growth

partne

Our management is inspired

to provide flexible solutions

to meet our customer

changing r

in novate

We employ innovative

and winning strategies to

exceed our customers' and

shareholders' expectations.

  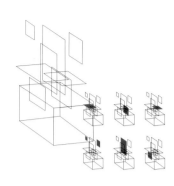

SANMINA-SCI

Systems
Process
Intension

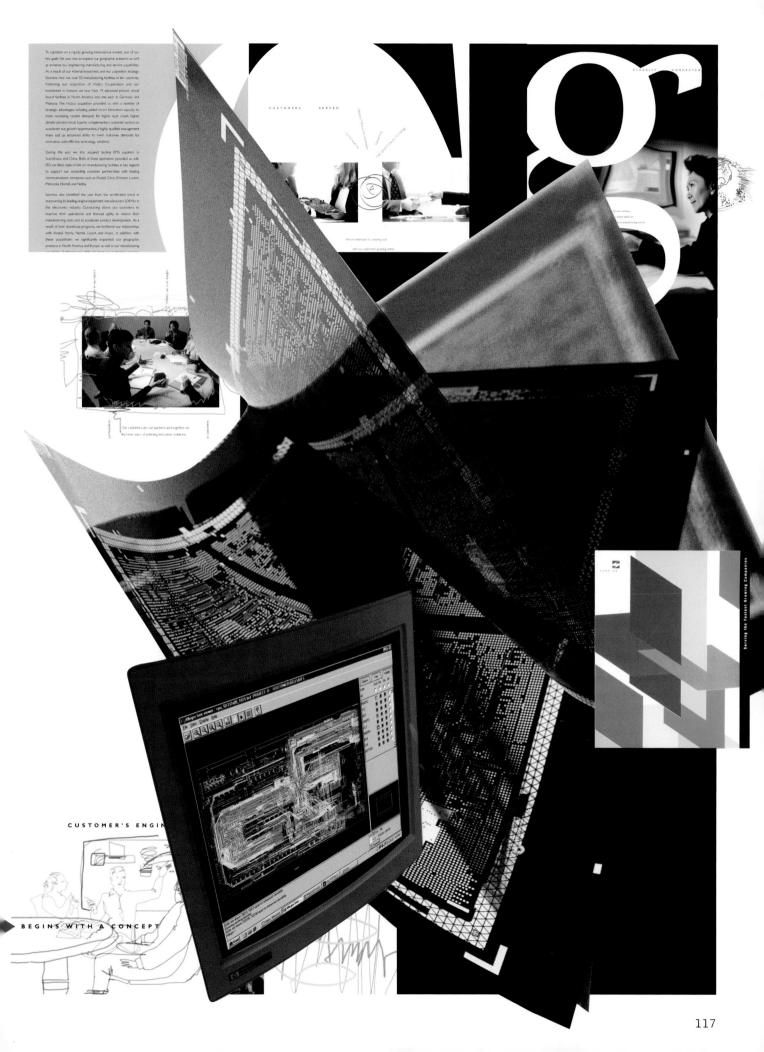

To capitalize on a rapidly growing international market, one of our key goals this year was to expand our geographic presence as well as enhance our engineering, manufacturing and service capabilities. As a result of our internal investment and our acquisition strategy, Sanmina now has over 50 manufacturing facilities in ten countries. Following our acquisition of Hadco Corporation and our investment in Inboard, we now have 15 advanced printed circuit board facilities in North America and one each in Germany and Malaysia. The Hadco acquisition provided us with a number of strategic advantages, including added circuit fabrication capacity to meet increasing market demands for higher layer count, higher density printed circuit boards; complementary customer sectors to accelerate our growth opportunities; a highly qualified management team; and an enhanced ability to meet customer demands for innovative, cost-effective technology solutions.

During the year we also acquired leading EMS suppliers in Scandinavia and China. Both of these operations provided us with ISO-certified, state-of-the-art manufacturing facilities in key regions to support our expanding customer partnerships with leading communications companies such as Alcatel, Cisco, Ericsson, Lucent, Motorola, Nortel and Nokia.

Sanmina also benefited this year from the accelerated trend in outsourcing by leading original equipment manufacturers (OEMs) in the electronics industry. Outsourcing allows our customers to improve their operational and financial agility, to reduce their manufacturing costs and to accelerate product development. As a result of their divestiture programs, we furthered our relationships with Alcatel, Harris, Nortel, Lucent, and Avaya. In addition, with these acquisitions we significantly expanded our geographic presence in North America and Europe, as well as our manufacturing capabilities. Furthermore, our ability to meet our customers' needs for

CUSTOMERS SERVED

CUSTOMER'S ENGIN

BEGINS WITH A CONCEPT

117

Libera Design Inc.

UCLA

S u m m e r   S e s s i o n s

The Fire

Logic
Life
Flexible

0
0
2

The Water

www.summer.ucla.edu

The Air

Performance
Balance
Precision

Libera Design has earned a reputation over 20 years of providing superior custom designed products. Our success is due to building long-term relationships with our clients and being an intregal part of building their image and wealth.

The Earth

Defenders of Freedom

NAF El Centro Air Show

Featuring the
Blue Angels

March 9, 2002

Brad Furr racing

Passion Invention
Vision Systems
Process Intension
Reaching Explosive
Flexibility Inspiring
Consistency Elegance
Nature Existence
Peace Time Interest
Rules Goals Special
Organize Cycles
Possibilities Innovate
Future Beyond Run
Play Wonder Awe

active design that
grows business
expands images
sets examples
makes a difference

Libera

Ph.D
1524a Cloverfield Boulevard
Santa Monica, California 90404
310.829.0900 fax 310.829.1859
www.phdla.com

Ph.D

Ph.D is a design office providing image development, identity systems and marketing materials to innovative companies in consumer products, high technology services and advertising. Our visual wit and ability to deliver large ideas in well-crafted detail enables our clients to do what they do better.

2

3

1. Developer conference poster
2. Alex Goes clothing company identity
3. Alex Goes clothing tag

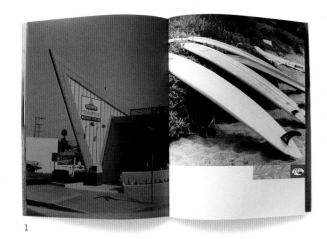

1

2

3

4

5

6

7

1,6. Quiksilver brand book

2. Photographer's identity

3-4. Dickson's promo book

5. Photographer's promo

7. Foundation Press sticker

8. Developmentor course book series

9. Alex Goes Fall marketing piece

10. Eames Primer book

11-12. Alex Goes Spring marketing piece

13. QuiksilverEdition identity

14. Cookbook

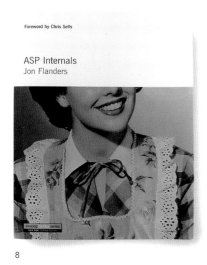

Foreword by Chris Sells

ASP Internals
Jon Flanders

8

9

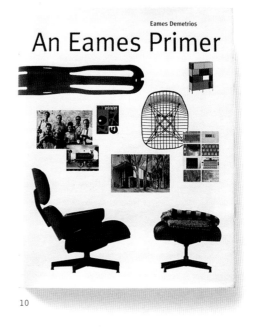

Eames Demetrios

An Eames Primer

10

alexgoes

11

alex goes

12

QUIKSILVE
VEREDITION

13

asianvegetables

Sara Deseran

14

1

eight/inspired.

ANN FIELD: brancusi, bird, hermes squares, chappie. danny kaye movies, matisse, jean-michel frank and a very tall designer. **BILL PHELPS:** eyes, wheels, strand, silence.... fallingwater, shifting sands, zuzu's petals and the isle of man tt.

HANNES SCHMID: wenders, eno, harleys, helmut lang. madonna, plastic, polke and sushi.

PAUL WEARING: the specials, chihuly, marvin gaye, gehry. vic and bob, miles davis, selmer saxophones and my life as a dog. **SCOGIN MAYO:** koolhaus, bauhaus, early bowie, late nights, pawson, jill, jungle and doctor no. **JOCK McDONALD:** russians, cubans, eccentrics, eskimos, surfers, japanese, elvis impersonators and everything in between.

GISELLE POTTER: pee-wee herman, cirque du soleil, roald dahl, mr. ed. tim burton, beatrix potter, harry potter and scout in to kill a mockingbird.

GEOF KERN: jacques tati, marcel broodthaers, outerbridge, buster keaton, tom and jerry, the stones, guy bourdin and vermeer. **JAMES NOEL SMITH:** newspapers, riesling kabinett, afternoon naps and tennessee. pick-ups, chainsaws, lawrence of arabia and dostoyevski. **TIM SIMMONS:** the man from u.n.c.l.e., bangers and mash, bang...

2

3

1. Foundation Press truck signage
2. Friend & Johnson promo book
3. DNA product packaging

1

stımmüng

2

3

énergie

4

TALENT
ENTERTAINMENT GROUP

7

ÜRBIT

8

FATHER'S
OFFICE

5

6

9

MOXLY

10

X-1

11

SCHNABEL

12

14

1. Office furniture
2. Sound editing
3. Commercials production
4. Lighting distribution
5,6. Neighborhood bar
7. Talent agents
8. Film production
9. Developmentor brand icons
10. Beauty guide
11. Commercials production
12. Musicologist/Francophile
13. SilverEdition clothing
14. Alex Goes clothing
15. Film production
16. Industrial lighting

QUIKSILVER

13

12C

15

FOCAL
POINT®

16

2325 Third Street
Suite 220
San Francisco, CA 94107
tel 415.255.6100
fax 415.255.6300
www.okitadesign.com

YASHI OKITA DESIGN

Yashi Okita Design was founded almost 20 years by a man with a mission; create beautiful design without sacrificing the message. Design is about communication. A good looking cover/logo/package doesn't mean anything if no intrinsic information can be drawn from the piece.

This is only one of the factors driving Yashi Okita. For him design is a passion, "When you pour your heart and soul into a project it will never be wrong". Whether the client is a Mom and Pop startup or a time-honored corporation, YOD gives 150%.

For the last couple of years YOD has been working with the High-Tech industry, although YOD is not exclusive. The company loves to create an entire visual "look" for their clients.

The designs on the following pages show how YOD has produced whole corporate ID programs that include creating the logo, business collateral, packaging, and to the website including the e-commerce.

BLACKSTONE:

The project was created to build a brand identity for an e-commerce business. This virtual store needs to have a strong, bold presence much like the coffee it represents. On a visual level, the logo illustrates the Hawaiian origins of the Kona coffee. The etching of the palm tree and volcano illustrate the traditional BlackStone Estate as tropical paradise were coffee flourishes. The classic swash type treatment unites the high-end product accomplishing an easy-to-understand cohesive package.

The intent of the design was to convey the charming environment of Hawaii and the delicious aroma of 100% Kona coffee. The overall presentation allows the customer to take their experience home with them.

1. Blackstone Coffee Company Logo

2. Hi and Low End Package Label

3. Stationary (Letterhead, #10 Envelope, and Business card

4. Website: Home page

5. Splash page

6. How to Brew page

7. Catalog page

1

2

BRUKER DALTONICS

The focus of the printed corporate marketing pieces was to maintain Bruker Daltonics' position as a leader in the life sciences industry. The brochure covers were created as part of a family for each instrument the company produces. The web site interprets and combines the same look and feel as the printed pieces with the interactivity of the Internet.

1. Sample Website pages
2. Presentation Folder and Product Brochures

TERABLAZE

Speed, movement, innovation, and technology were all-important components in the development of this logo for a Silicon Valley start up. The translation of the innovative theme was introduced on to the web site by the use of abstract images, vivid color and bold type. The stationary system has a traditional straightforward design to show how a new company will have an establish look and feel.

1. Stationary (Letterhead, #10 Envelope and 2 sided Business Card
2. TeraBlaze Logo
3. Sample Website Pages

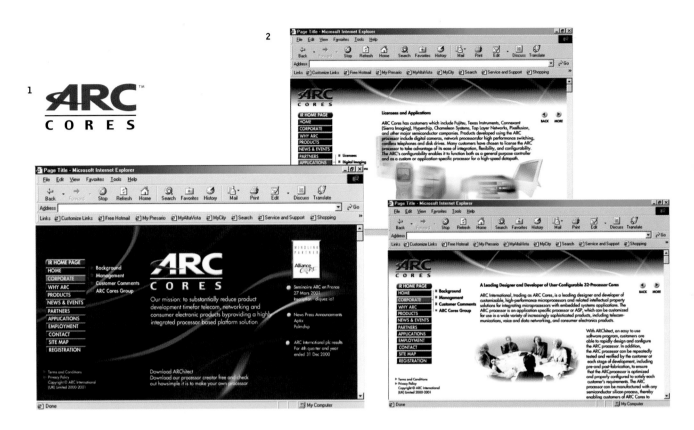

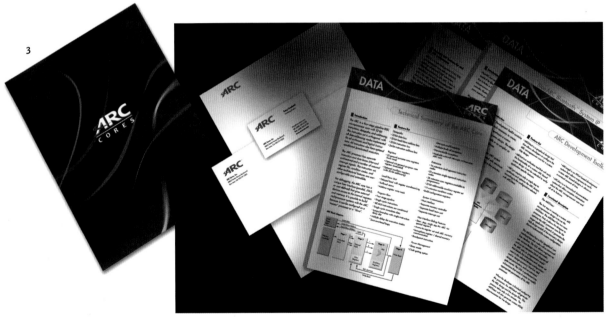

ARC CORES

The objective was to design an identity system for ARC Cores, which would be, contemporary, have longevity and even have adaptability. The innovative spirit of the company is represented with the moving ribbons integrated in the stationary system and web site.

1. ARC Cores Logo
2. Sample Website Pages
3. Presentation Folder
2. Stationary and Datasheets

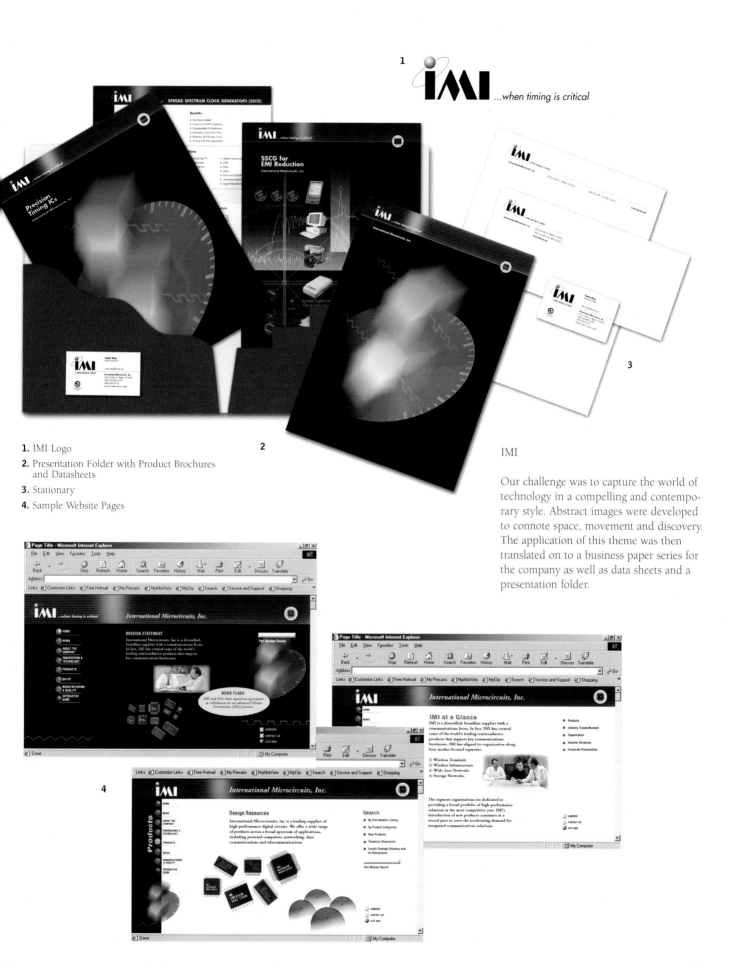

1. IMI Logo
2. Presentation Folder with Product Brochures and Datasheets
3. Stationary
4. Sample Website Pages

IMI

Our challenge was to capture the world of technology in a compelling and contemporary style. Abstract images were developed to connote space, movement and discovery. The application of this theme was then translated on to a business paper series for the company as well as data sheets and a presentation folder.

GADZOOX

Gadzoox Networks provides an intelligent networking infra-structure for storage and data management with scalable, interoperable appliances and switches. Duo-tone photos of people who make up the company provided the annual report theme, emphasizing opportunity, momentum, and optimism for growth and development of innovative products for corporate community systems.

Gadzoox 2000 Corporate Backgrounder Brochure

Introducing Integraph Media...

The internet and especially e-commerce has provided new opportunities for design. Wanting to stay viable in this cyber-market, Yashi Okita Design formed Integraph media with Dux Raymond Sy of Quantum X several years ago. Integraph Media is a new kind of web design company. It combines the experience of Yashi Okita design with the cutting edge technology of Quantum X to create innovative and productive interactive publications.

Integraph Media offers web design and development solutions to meet each business objective. They will assist clients throughout the web development lifecycle. From con-ceptualization to deployment to site analysis, their goal is to give the best return on investment.

Web services include:

Web Development
Site maintenance and Management
Internet Marketing
Intranet development
Web Usability Testing
New Media Deployment
E-commerce

At the core of Integraph Media is the combined strength of seasoned professional from diverse and technology backgrounds working hard to help you unlock the value of your enterprise and prepare you for what's next on the business horizon.

With the addition of Integraph Media, YOD has been able to design entire corporate identity programs for clients.

Warren Group Graphic Design
8695 Washington Blvd. Suite 210
Culver City, California 90232
310.204.4012
www.studiodeluxe.com

1

WARREN GROUP / STUDIO DELUXE

What is deluxe? Nearly two decades in the making, the graphic design team at Warren Group has launched Studio Deluxe, a space worthy of the design principles it was founded upon—collaboration, creativity and wit. Located in Culver City's historic Beacon Laundry Building, Warren Group is the ideal place to be when you want outstanding communication solutions that can distinguish your message in a busy world.

Originally founded in Venice, USA in 1984, Warren Group has built a reputation for organic design solutions and an enviable client list to match it. With the introduction of new members to its creative graphic team, a move to a "deluxe" space that mirrored its artistic sensibility became essential. Thus, early in 2002, Warren Group moved into the renovated Beacon Laundry Building, a once bustling commercial laundry in 1930's Los Angeles. Taking inspiration from its new space, the graphic design team redesigned its own identity system in a style it has dubbed "Laundry Chic." From revamping stationary and promotional materials, Warren Group even hosted the unveiling of Studio Deluxe with an eclectic event cleverly deemed, "Hoe Down & Dirty."

The firm's transformation reflects its willingness to embrace change. After all, reinventing organizational identities is just one of the many tasks performed daily at Warren Group. It lends its strategic thinking to print collateral, brand identity, packaging, advertising, and web design. But what attracts clients isn't a list of services, but the firm's experience, dedication and collaborative philosophy. "What I appreciate most about Warren Group is that I always feel like I am a part of the creative process," says one long-time client.

The collaborative renovation of Warren Group is just the latest example of the classic, yet irreverent style that has helped the firm compete for major clients against others many times its size. Included in its resume are such names as Disney/ABC, University of Southern California, Mattel, Childrens Hospital Los Angeles, Heritage Worldwide Sports, and the Capital Group Companies. In addition, Warren Group's award-winning designs are included in the permanent design collection of the United States Library of Congress. As its own identity continues to evolve, Warren Group prepares to enter its 19th successful year by assisting a host of new clients with diverse communication strategies. Some things never change.

2

4

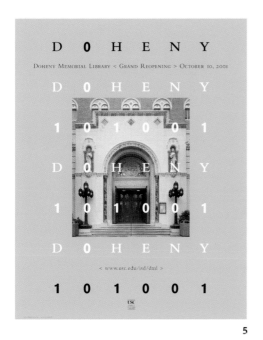

5

1. Previous spread: Beacon Laundry Building at night
2. Previous spread: Studio Deluxe promotional materials
3. Merchandise system, Doheny Memorial Library
4. Bibliotech_USC magazine, USC Information Services
5. Grand reopening poster, Doheny Memorial Library

THE SCHOOL OF ENGINEERING IS AT THE CENTER OF USC'S
EFFORTS TO CREATE NEW PARADIGMS FOR RESPONDING TO THE
MOST IMPORTANT PROBLEMS AND OPPORTUNITIES OF THE 21ST
CENTURY. EXCITING NEW TECHNOLOGIES BEING DEVELOPED IN THE
SCHOOL PROVIDE THE FOUNDATION FOR MUCH OF OUR WORK ON
A BROAD SPECTRUM OF SOCIAL AND TECHNOLOGICAL ISSUES.
DR. LLOYD ARMSTRONG, JR. | PROVOST AND SENIOR VICE PRESIDENT FOR ACADEMIC AFFAIRS
UNIVERSITY OF SOUTHERN CALIFORNIA

chemical engineering

6

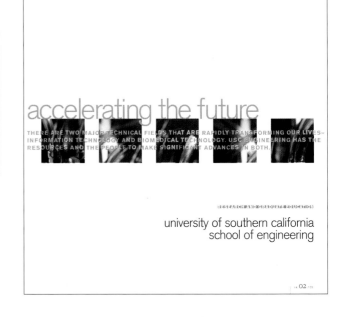

accelerating the future

THERE ARE TWO MAJOR TECHNICAL FIELDS THAT ARE RAPIDLY TRANSFORMING OUR LIVES—
INFORMATION TECHNOLOGY AND BIOMEDICAL TECHNOLOGY. USC ENGINEERING HAS THE
RESOURCES AND THE PEOPLE TO MAKE SIGNIFICANT ADVANCES IN BOTH.

university of southern california
school of engineering

serenity springs

larta

KNOW
POOL
EDGE

7   **8**   **9**   **10**

13

HERITAGE
WORLD WIDE SPORTS
2002

11   **12**

14

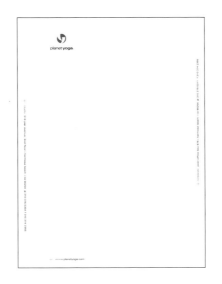

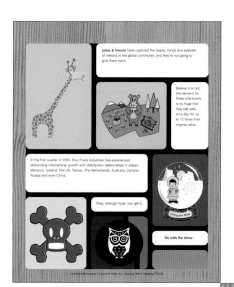

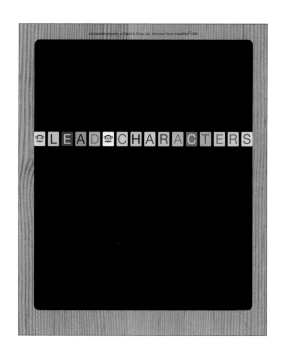

15

14. Identity system, Planet Yoga
15. Media pitchbook, Zeros & Ones, Inc./paul frank

16

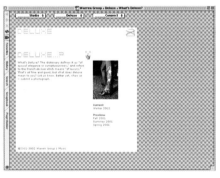

17

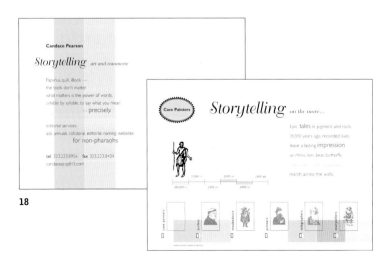

18

16. Studio opening invitation, Warren Group/Studio Deluxe
17. Web site, Warren Group/Studio Deluxe
18. Promotional postcard series, Candace Pearson,
    the Writers' Project

2525 Main Street, Suite 204
Santa Monica, California 90405
310_396_7724>voice
310_396_1686>fax
studio@loueyrubino.com
New York_Hong Kong

LOUEY/RUBINO DESIGN GROUP

Founded in 1984, Louey/Rubino Design Group is based in Santa Monica with satellite offices in New York City and Hong Kong. A winner of nearly 300 international communication arts awards, Louey/Rubino Design Group is a full-service marketing communications firm specializing in image and identity, corporate communications and related promotional and advertising programs. The firm offers Fortune 500 companies and major brands professional assistance in creating comprehensive programs that solve complex communications challenges on time and within budget.

The varied backgrounds, interests and professional qualifications of Louey/Rubino Design Group's management team and staff have given the company top-level experience in many arenas including strategic planning, marketing communications, corporate communications and identity, package design, space planning, public relations, executive communications and related promotional and advertising initiatives. All projects, whether on-going programs or project-based initiatives, are given the utmost personal attention.

The firm has had the pleasure to serve many leading corporations including KB Home, Lexus, Mandarin Oriental, Hyatt International, Marriott, St. Regis Hotels and Resorts, MCI/Worldcom, Price Waterhouse Coopers, Mercedes Benz, Morgan Stanley, The Walt Disney Company, SunAmerica and Tumi.

Louey/Rubino Design Group's work is included in the United States Library of Congress Permanent Collection and has been featured in Graphis, Interiors Magazine, Print, How, Communication Arts, The James Beard Awards, The Mead Show, the AR100, the Potlatch Annual Report Show, the American Institute of Graphic Arts, Printing Industries Association and The Type Director's Club.

POOL**BAR+GRILL**

POLARIS

CRUST

SEIDNER
& COMPANY

Investment Management

elements

GAUCIN

CHIANTI
ORGANIC DINING

CLUB NINETEEN

MONARCH

Restaurant_NoMI_Park Hyatt Chicago / Promotional Brochure_Lithographix

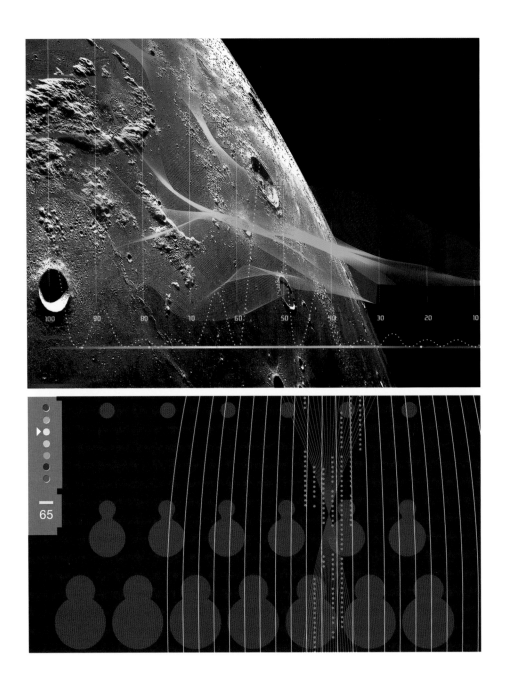

Poster Campaign

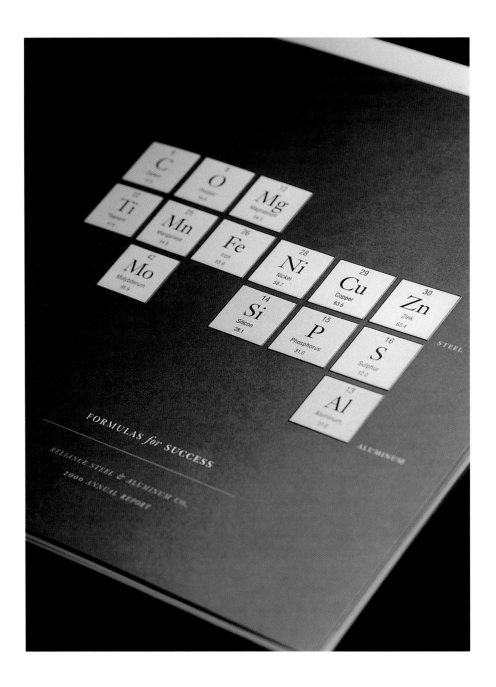

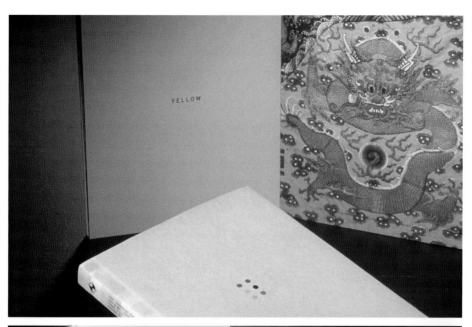

Promotional Brochure_Foundation Press / Annual Report_KB Home

inform   inspire   identify

The Designory *inc.*
211 East Ocean Boulevard, Suite 100
Long Beach, California 90802-4809
562.624.0200
www.designory.com

THE DESIGNORY *INC.*

We'll admit it. We love cars. Now that we've gotten that out of the way, here are a few other things you should know about The Designory *inc.* We're located in downtown Long Beach. We've done work on everything from architectural lighting and satellite radio to mountain bikes and ski resorts. But when it does come to our automotive accounts, we work with TBWA\Chiat\Day, Goodby Silverstein & Partners and Merkley Newman Harty. So yes, we know how to roll up our sleeves and collaborate with the big boys. (Very important when it comes to maintaining a brand's distinctive voice and strategic landing approach.) But, most importantly, the craftsmen/women who work here thrive on the creative process, embrace the power of design and evangelize the concept of *transmedia communications.* Or, in other words, "the seamless, holistic integration of ideas where nothing gets lost in the translation." That means the big idea gets to the right people at the right time in the most effective medium. It also means a streamlined message that's integrated and linked. Not merely duplicated. From Web site, environmental, interactive, outdoor, print, package, database design and exhibit to POP, direct marketing, even video or film. On occasion, we've even been known to do a car brochure or two.

1

2

3

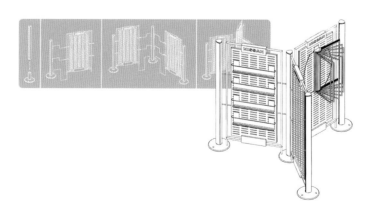

2002 Nissan North America transmedia elements

1. Nissan Altima brochure with CD-ROM.

2. Nissan Altima CD-ROM. One very media-rich experience.

3. Nissan showroom environmental hardware, graphics and application.

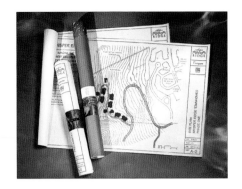

1

2

Horst Leitner

CARBON·FIBER

3

Horst Leitner Design

B4

B4

AMP RESEARCH

Graphics, web and other transmedia

1. The Canyons Resort / Whisper Ridge sales packaging, direct mail campaign, identity and resort book.

2. Pie.com Web site, an on-line action sports community portal for adrenaline junkies.

3. AMP Research mountain bike identity, promotional materials and bike graphics.

1

2

3

4

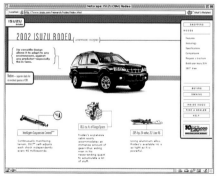

5

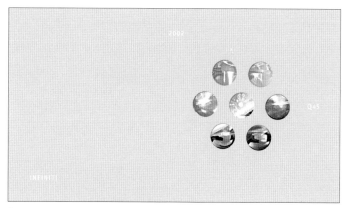

6

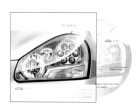

7

2002 Isuzu transmedia elements

1. Autoshow panels.
2. Full-line SUV brochure.
3. Joe Isuzu air freshener.
4. Autoshow video.
5. Corporate Web site.

2002 Infiniti transmedia elements

6. Infiniti Q45 launch brochure.
7. Infiniti Q45 pre-launch CD-ROM.

TRANSMEDIA IS?

a) The signage found on highways, freeways and interstates.

b) A music television station from Transylvania.

c) A way of linking various forms of communication together with consistency, brought to you by The Designory *inc.*

Free donuts on Tuesdays and Thursdays.

Smullen Design
85 N. Raymond Avenue • Suite 280
Pasadena, California 91103

voice. 626.405.0886
fax. 626.405.1443

www.smullendesign.com
staff@smullendesign.com

SMULLEN DESIGN

Smullen Design was founded in 1990 with a single objective: to deliver effective, creative marketing solutions for corporate, entertainment and new media clientele. Today, the firm is a recognized leader in branding, corporate communication & identity programs, and strategic theming & concept development. Smullen's award-winning work for Fortune 500 accounts, including Cigna Healthcare, Farmers Insurance, General Motors and Lockheed, has helped nurture a creative atmosphere where inspiration, insight and experience lead the creative process. Smullen's early vision has resulted in a stimulating, creative environment where a team of highly-motivated professionals, what Smullen calls the "Creative Core," produce designs that continue to break new ground.

A unique solution to the conventional, large agency "Account Team" approach, the Creative Core matches the principal's experience with the specialized skills of a core staff of professionals. On selected projects, the Creative Core is complemented by out-sourcing more specialized and highly technical skills.

These methods are reflected in recent work for Disney Imagineering, Edison International, Harvey Entertainment, Universal, Viacom and Warner Bros.

Maureen Smullen, a graduate of Art Center College of Design and a former senior designer for the national agency J. Walter Thompson, is keenly aware of her client's needs. Currently, she's involved with various corporate marketing communications projects, the branding of entertainment & retail venues and the development of new consumer products. Her long roster of successfully completed projects and unparalleled design organization continue to present trademark solutions for clients in search of consummate creativity in a fast-changing, highly competitive marketing environment.

"Creativity excites
the consumer, enlivens
the marketplace and
stimulates success!"

~ Maureen Smullen

Barbie Avenue Furniture, Mattel

A line of sophisticated furniture designed to reflect the Barbie lifestyle. The five-piece collection, evocative of the Barbie brand, culture and sensibility, captures the personality of the beloved icon through its well-crafted design.

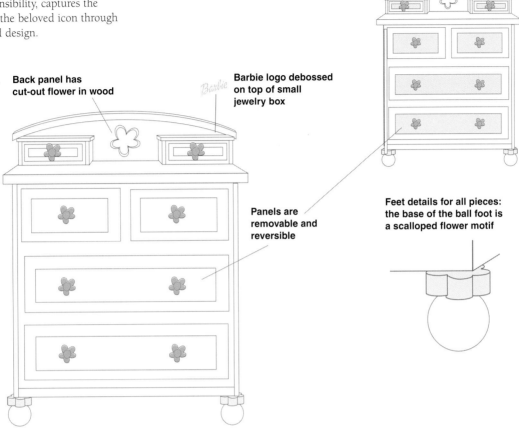

Back panel has cut-out flower in wood

Barbie logo debossed on top of small jewelry box

Panels are removable and reversible

Feet details for all pieces: the base of the ball foot is a scalloped flower motif

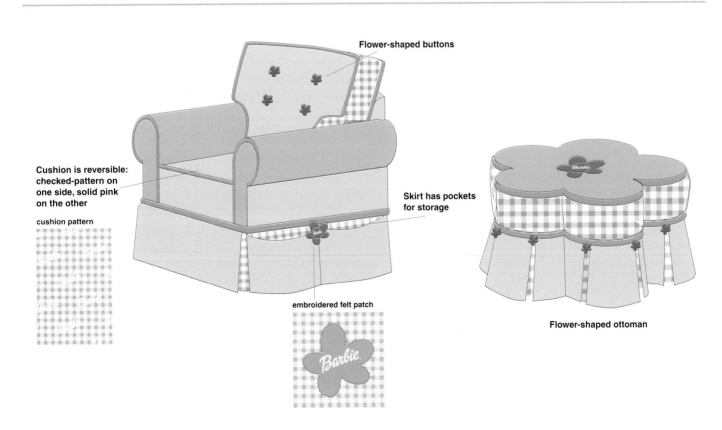

Flower-shaped buttons

Cushion is reversible: checked-pattern on one side, solid pink on the other

cushion pattern

Skirt has pockets for storage

embroidered felt patch

Flower-shaped ottoman

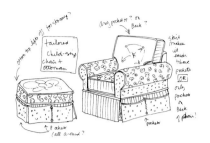

Tabletop Side 1:
Play mat added to make
Barbie™ playhouse

Tabletop Side 2:
Game board

Table top is
removable/reversible

Drawer for
storage
of play mat,
game pieces,
art supplies, etc

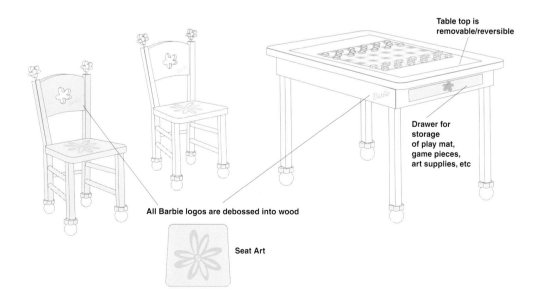

All Barbie logos are debossed into wood

Seat Art

**The Mummy Animated Series,
Style Guide, Universal Studios**

Inspired by the drama and excitement in the
successful feature films, Smullen's style guide
for The Mummy animated series was designed
to give Universal Home Entertainment the tools
to help licensees bring the story and characters
to life through a variety of products and media.

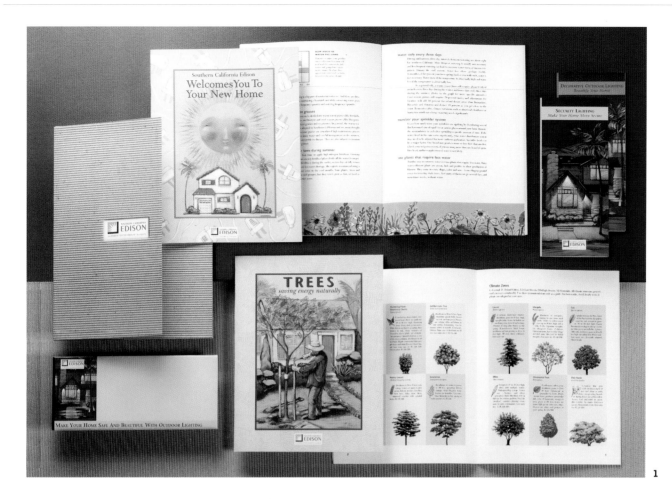

1. Southern California Edison,
   Consumer Marketing Campaign
2. Time Warner Interactive,
   Endorfun Packaging and Collateral
3. Warner Bros.,
   Harry Potter shopping bag
4. Warner Bros.,
   Scooby-Doo shopping bag
5. Mann Theatres,
   Chinese Theatre shopping bag

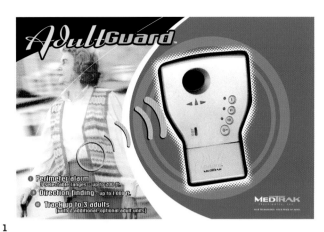

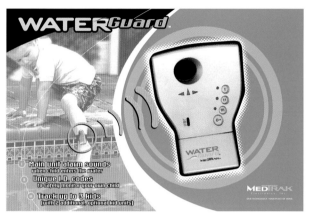

MedTrack Electronics, Inc.

1. Consumer Packaging
2. Brand Identities
3. Identity System / Sell Sheets
4. Brand Standards Manual

1

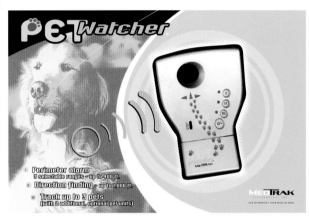

2

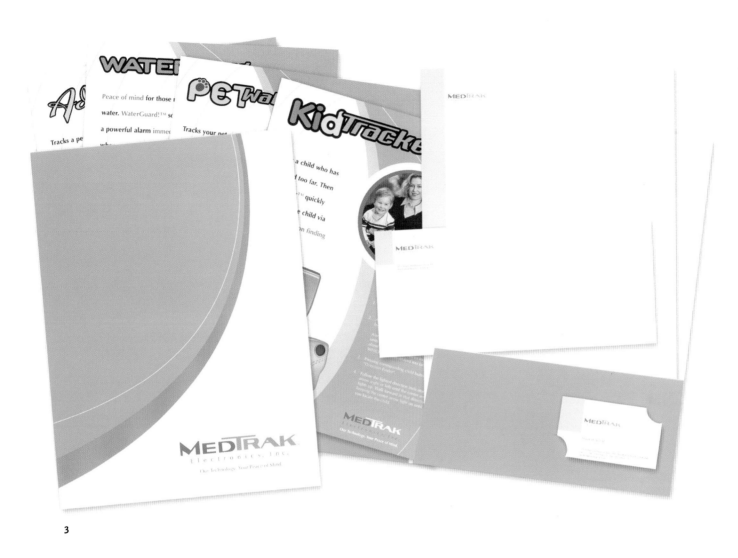

3

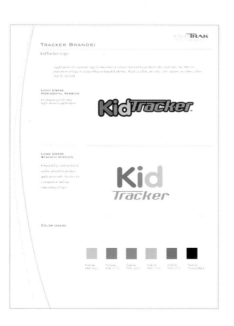

4

1

2

3

4

5

6

7

8

9

10

11

1. Paseo Colorado

2. Warner Bros. Studio Store NYC

3. Warner Bros. Stage 16 Restaurant

4. Tower I.D. Medical

5. American Telemarketing Association

6. MCA / Universal Studios

7. Sunset Strip

8. West Hollywood Convention & Visitors

9-11. Mann's Chinese Theatre

Visual Asylum
205 West Date Street
San Diego, California 92101
Tel.619.233.9633
Fax.619.233.9637
maelinl@visualasylum.com
www.visualasylum.com

VISUAL ASYLUM

Growing up in Leadville, Colorado, sisters MaeLin and Amy Levine lived big adventures horseback riding in the Rockies, camping out under the stars and dreaming of what was to come. It was a magical time and a magical place, and they were convinced, as children often are, that anything was possible. The sisters grew up, each following her own dream, one in Denver and the other in Kansas City. Eventually their dreams brought them together again, this time in San Diego, where for fourteen years they have worked side by side in their grown-up adventure, Visual Asylum.

MaeLin and Amy were determined to create a working environment for themselves that captured the magic of their childhood. They wanted it to be a motivating place for them to work and an inspiring place for people to visit. The result is a turn-of-the-century boarding house filled with bright colors and whimsical, custom-made furniture that captures the spirit and enthusiasm of the people who occupy it.

For their clients, partnering with Visual Asylum means a chance to create a "visual language", a system of communication incorporating color, typography, illustration and photography, that mirrors not just the identity of the client, but the energy and interests of the target audience. Then, with the help of their six person staff, friends really, they implement the visual languages, creating executions that match facts and information with smart design solutions that touch people and connect them to their own dreams, filling them with a sense of adventure and the magic of possibility.

1

4

2

1. Logo
2. Stationery System
3. Business Card Promos
4. New Client Welcome Gift Box
5. Mouse Pad
6. Environment
7. Promotional T-shirts
8. Holiday Client Gifts
9. KooKoo Holiday Client Gift
10. Website
11. Environment

5

3

6

7

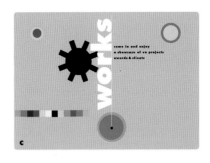

8

9

10

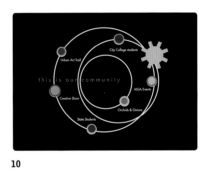

11

1

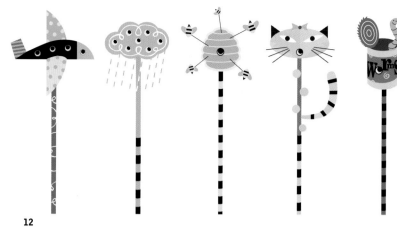

12

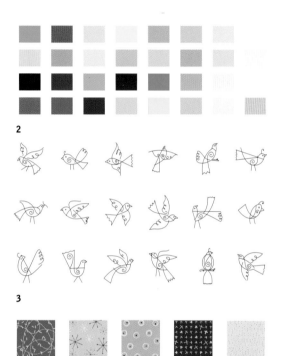

2

3

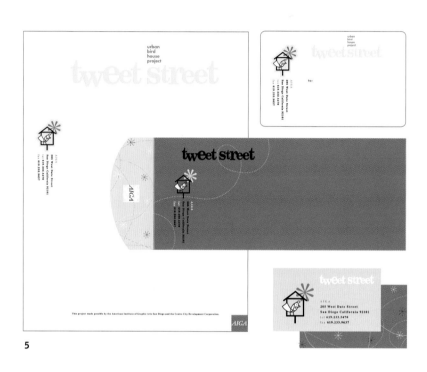

5

6

8

7

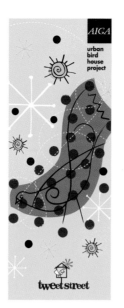

9

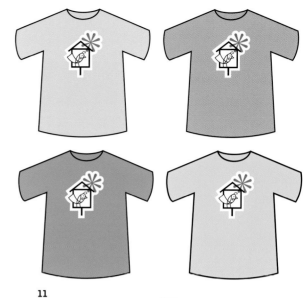

11

10

Tweet Street

Since Tweet Street is a bird park in an area of urban redevelopment with few other open green spaces, our challenge was to make it both inviting and fun as well as educational. Inspired by the unusual birdhouses created for the park, we developed a playful name, bright color palette and whimsical illustrative style to set the tone for the type of experience visitors to the park can expect to have. These elements work together to generate enthusiasm for the project and convey educational information while reinforcing a distinct identity for Tweet Street.

Side View   **Front View**
← entry hole

12

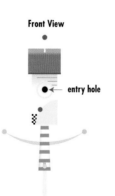

Front View   **Side View**
entry hole →
bird bath
feeder

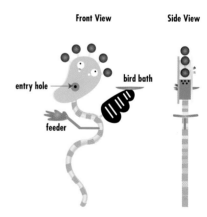

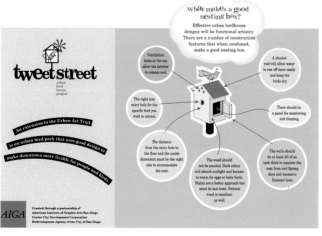

13

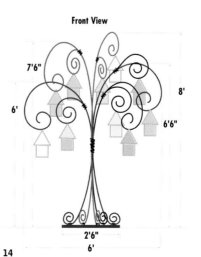

14

1. Logo
2. Color Palette
3. Bird Illustrations
4. Patterns
5. Stationery System
6. Product: Note Cards
7. Promotional Poster
8. Special Awards
9. Banners
10. Show Opening Invitation
11. Product: T-Shirts
12. Bird House Design
13. Display Graphics
14. Display Design

1

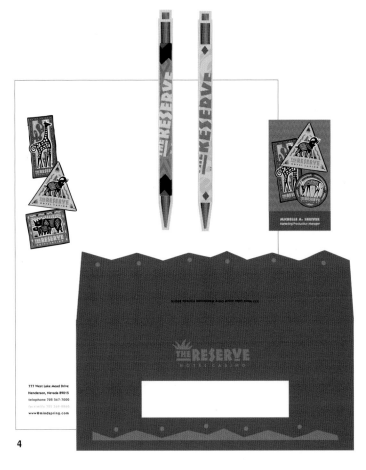

4

2

The Reserve Hotel Casino

The Reserve is comprised of a hotel, casino, six restaurants and three bars, so our challenge was to give each venue in this gamer's paradise its own identity, while remaining true to the encompassing African safari theme. Based on the unique character attributes of each venue, we created a series of logos for them that work both independently and as a group. Through their many applications, these identities made for a cohesive presentation while generating a sense of adventure as visitors visit the many regions of The Reserve Hotel Casino.

5

3

6

1. Identity System
   Logotype, Logo Collection
2. Color Palette
3. Illustrative Patterns/Textures
4. Stationery System
5. Matches
6. Chips and Tokens
7. Hotel Room Amenities Package
8. Employee Recruitment Signage
9. Restaurant Signage
10. Restaurant, Outlet Identities

7

8

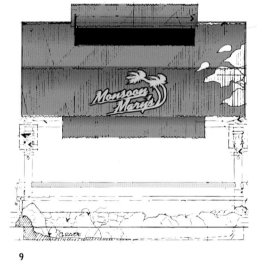

9

10

1

2

3

5

6

4

7

Women First HealthCare

Women First markets products and services to both women at mid-life and their physicians, so our challenge was to effectively reach two different demographics. Informed by research, we made a strategic decision to focus on active, vital women at work and play rather than the traditional, sedentary image of older women. We developed fresh photographic and illustrative imagery, a unique color palette and elegant typography and implemented them consistently and comprehensively to establish a strong brand character for Women First HealthCare.

1. Logo
2. Color Palette
3. Custom Photographic Image Library
4. Custom Illustration Library
5. Website
6. Consumer Product Identity and Packaging
7. Print Collateral Materials

6

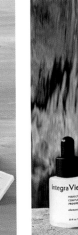

6

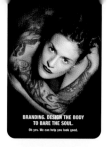

Boardwalk
116 N. Maryland Ave.
Suite 220
Glendale, California 91206
818.566.7007
www.boardwalk.la

BOARDWALK

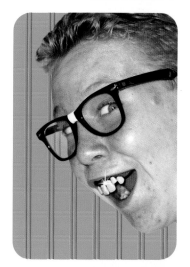

Boardwalk is a full-service
design agency that specializes
in developing brand identities
for entertainment properties.

Founded in 1990, Boardwalk
has helped propel major brands
across the nation and around
the world. Our consulting and
design services make us a
favorite industry resource,
known for on-target branding,
killer creative, professional
execution and attentive service.

To every project, whether
massive or microscopic, we
bring sound strategic thinking,
a passion for excellence and
the all-too-rare conviction that
entertainment design should
be entertaining in its own right.

(Previous page)
Series of self-promotional postcards

1

2

3

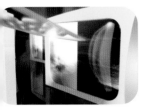

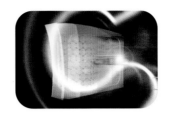

1. Brand identity and 10 sec. spot for Channel Surfing
2. Identity and CD packaging for The Excello Story
3. Brand identity for Santa Monica Pier
4. Style and branding guides for Honda Racing
5A-B. Graphics for Honda Racing brand
6. Style guide for Honda Racing
7. Packaging for Honda Racing brand

1

2

3

4

1. Product catalog for Curious George brand
2. Launch/marketing kit for Playboy TV
3. Web site link for Pink Panther
4. Super Bowl XXXVI host city identity
5. 30 sec. spot for Tony Hawk, Inc.
6. Corporate identity and stationery ensemble for Tony Hawk, Inc.

5

6

1. Identity development and style guide for Sitting Ducks

2. Brand identity and 30 sec. spot for STAPLES Center

3. Identity development for The WB Network

4. Identity and style guide for Crash Bandicoot brand

5A-B. Graphics for Crash Bandicoot brand

6. Packaging for Crash Bandicoot brand

2

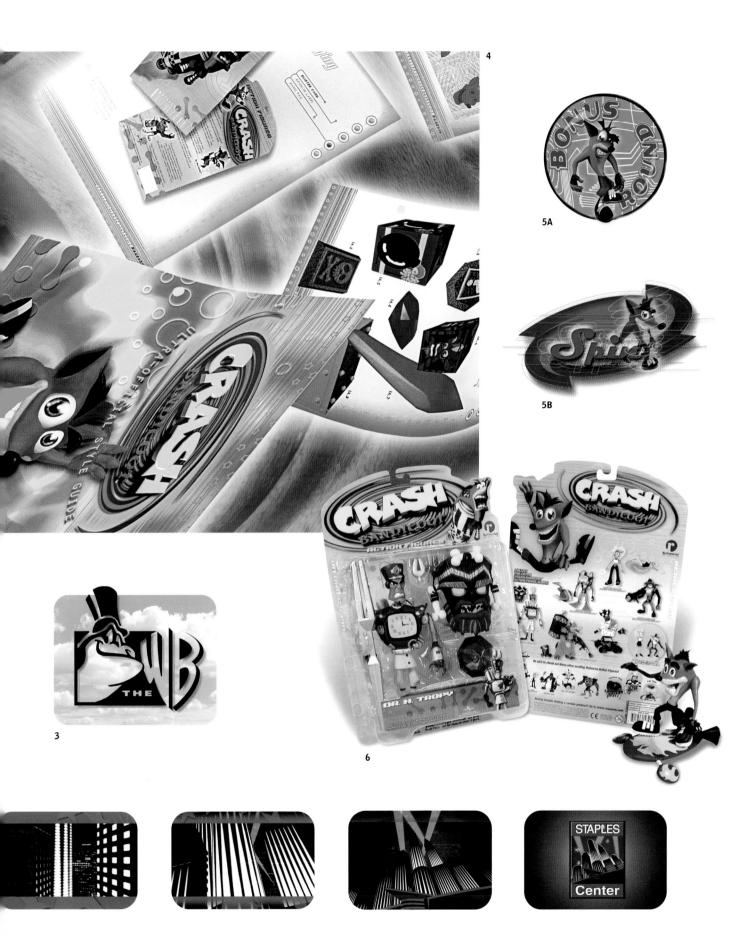

4

5A

5B

3

6

183

1

2

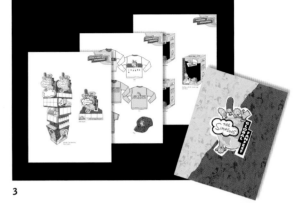

3

6

4

5

7

1. Brand identity for Spyro the Dragon
2. Promotional identity for the
   Los Angeles Dodgers
3. Style guide for Simpsons' Global Fanfest
4. Banners for Simpsons' Global Fanfest
5. Invitation to Simpsons licensees
6. Simpsons/Burger King promotion
7. Simpsons retail co-branding

Painting by Stephen Ludwig, founder, Group 22, Inc.

Group 22, Inc.
200 West Grand Avenue
El Segundo, California 90245
310.322.2210
studio@group22.com
www.group22.com

GROUP 22, INC.

El Segundo-based Group 22, Inc. was founded in 1996 under a different name and in the converted front bedroom of a house. It has since evolved into the growing firm that it is today with a deconstructivist 3,300 square foot studio and commands a full-time staff of seven. Rather than becoming a one-trick-pony, niche design studio, the work that Group 22 does spans many disciplines covering both digital and print media.

The principal designers at Group 22 share a combined experience in the field of over thirty years. However, Group 22 is a design collective in which all employees take part in the design of any particular project as well as the direction of the company.

There are no titles or hierarchy here; just a family.

The firm's philosophy is as simple as it is true; less is more. Design should first and foremost communicate and should never get in the way of the message.

At any particular Group 22 gathering you'll likely find a mix of vendors, clients and employees. The reason is because Group 22 likes to work in close partnership with their clients. Instead of doggedly presenting comps and sketches for approval or rejection, we feel that clients should be an integral part of the design process. Group 22 has many friends as clients and often turns clients into friends.

Whether you pass by the studio at two in the morning or eight o'clock at night, seven days a week, you will always find the lights on and at least one of us hard at work. Why? Quite simply put: We love what we do.

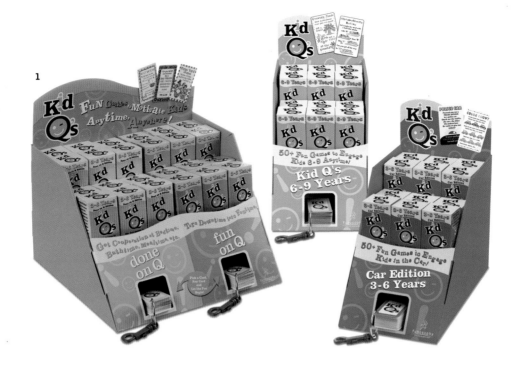

5

OneSource
S E R V I C E S

7

6

ATM/RIOnet

1. Kid Q's packaging
2. Group 22, Inc. Flash website
3. American Hot Rod Celebration logo
   for Ford Motor Cars
4. Montage Handcrafted Soap Company logo
5. Reality Check logo
6. ATM/RIOnet logo
7. One Source Services logo
8. Mercury Global freestanding display
9. The Palms Casino Playboy Mansion
   party invitation [front & back]

8

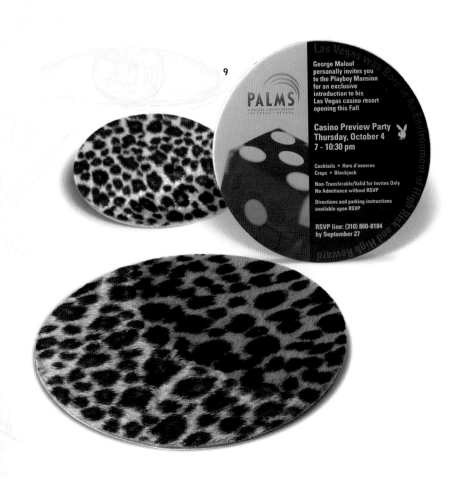

9

PALMS

George Maloof
personally invites you
to the Playboy Mansion
for an exclusive
introduction to his
Las Vegas casino resort
opening this Fall

Casino Preview Party
Thursday, October 4
7 - 10:30 pm

Cocktails • Hors d'oeuvres
Craps • Blackjack

Non-Transferable/Valid for Invitee Only
No Admittance without RSVP

Directions and parking instructions
available upon RSVP

RSVP line: (310) 860-8184
by September 27

1. Tow Finestone and Associates, LLC logo
2. U.S. Pro-Drive™ logo
3. Spa Mantra logo
4. DVD Entertainment Group Presskit
5. DVD Audio website
6. DVD Holiday Release CD-Rom

1

5

4

2

3

6

8

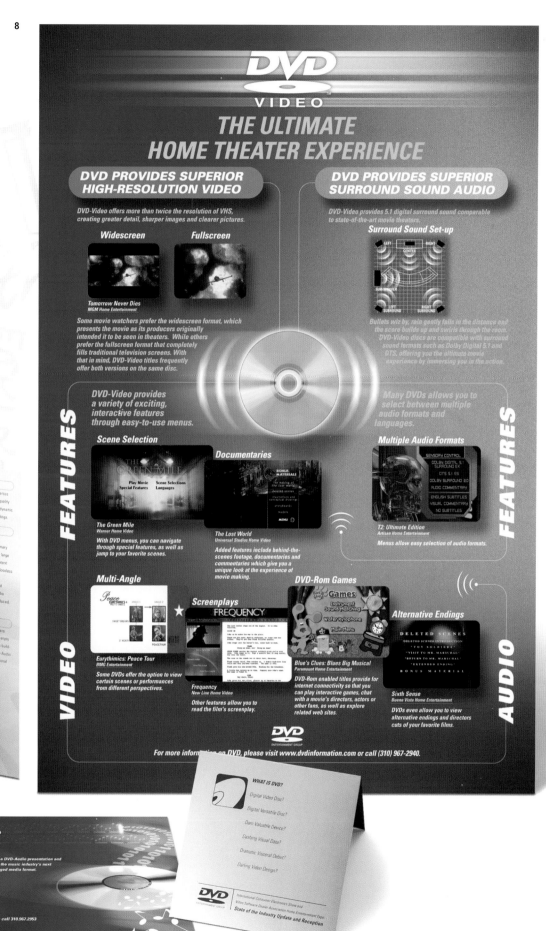

7

9

10

1. UCLA Santa Monica Medical Center website
2. Heal the Bay Annual Benefit Dinner program
3. Heal the Bay Annual Benefit Dinner invite
4. Mercury Media website
5. Beechnut website
6. Toyota Parts and Service Department collateral materials
7. Mesa Microwave website
8. Pacific Communications Group website
9. CO-OP Network 2001 Annual Report and CD-Rom

1

2

3

4

5

1. WaterBuddies packaging logo
2. Slap-On Art Decals logo
3. Eroticals packaging logo
4. WaterBuddies packaging
5. Slap-On Art Decals packaging

Cahan & Associates
171 Second Street, Fifth Floor
San Francisco, CA 94105
415.621.0915
www.cahanassociates.com

CAHAN & ASSOCIATES

Cahan & Associates possesses a unique ability for honing in on a singular, emotional truth that makes people care. While the San Francisco-based design agency is widely praised for its evocative annual reports, it has also gained significant recognition for its product packaging, brand identity, direct mail, advertising and web design. Whatever the creative challenge, the goal is the same: to peel away the marketing and expose the kernel of truth within.

To do so, the agency's founder and creative director, Bill Cahan, leads his designers on an intellectual journey into a client's business and challenges. Cahan's passion for fresh thinking is reflected in his team's commitment to doing hours and hours of research before a single design layout is attempted. It's the kind of in-depth analysis that clients often wish they had the time to do themselves—and it uncovers creative paths that are unique, original and quite often groundbreaking.

"Our range of solutions is varied because it reflects our client's message and culture, not our own," says Cahan, which helps explain not only the diversity of creative thinking at Cahan but also the diversity of clients. From Fortune 500 companies to emerging growth companies, from high tech and biotech leaders to sporting goods and dry goods makers—Cahan thrives on finding new problems to be solved. In large part because the agency's founder is so easily bored with repeating ideas and approaches.

That "impatience," as Cahan himself calls it, has fueled the agency's success for more than 18 years, a track record that includes winning over 2000 awards and write-ups in hundreds of periodicals and books. Cahan's penchant for refreshing the stodgy world of annual reports is being chronicled in Cahan & Associates on Annual Reports, due out from Rockport Publishers in Winter 2003. And Princeton Architectural Press has released a book on Cahan & Associates titled "I Am Almost Always Hungry," which is highly regarded among design professionals nationally and internationally.

By any measure, one word best sums up the work of Cahan & Associates: Smart. Time and again, Cahan and his staff have demonstrated that design driven by thoughtfulness is design that ends up being memorable.

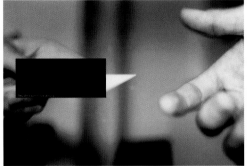

1

1. Gartner 2000 Annual Report. Creative director: Bill Cahan. Art directors: Bill Cahan, Kevin Roberson. Designer: Kevin Roberson. Photographers: Lars Tunbjork, Steven Ahlgren, Catherine Ledner. Illustrator: Steve Hussey. Copywriter: Tony Leighton.

2

2. PBS 1999 Annual Report. Creative director:
Bill Cahan. Art directors: Bill Cahan, Bob
Dinetz. Designer: Bob Dinetz. Photographers:
Ken Probst, Russell Johnson, William Short,
Paul Rocheleau, Suzanne Stack. Copywriters:
David Stone, Bob Dinetz, Tom Epstein,
Stu Kantor.

You have the opportunity to invest in the future of art in the Bay Area and to build the first American art museum that will realize the full potential of creating a museum in a park.

 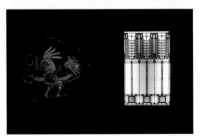

3

3. Fine Arts Museum, de Young Private Case.
Creative director: Bill Cahan. Art directors:
Bill Cahan, Michael Braley. Designer:
Michael Braley. Photographer: Environmental,
Christian Kerez; various stock images from
museum archives. Illustrator: Nanette Biers.
Copywriter: Linda Peterson.

S i m p l y S h e

4   5

6   7

8

4. Advanced Medicine Logo. Creative director: Bill Cahan. Art directors: Bill Cahan, Bob Dinetz. Designer: Bob Dinetz.

5. SimplyShe Logo. Creative director: Bill Cahan. Art directors: Bill Cahan, Sharrie Brooks. Designer: Sharrie Brooks.

6. Great Lodge Logo. Creative director: Bill Cahan. Designer: Neal Ashby.

7. Waterkeepers Logo. Creative director: Bill Cahan. Art directors: Bill Cahan, Michael Braley. Designer: Michael Braley.

8. Clif Bar Packaging. Creative director: Bill Cahan. Art directors: Bill Cahan, Bob Dinetz. Designer: Bob Dinetz. Illustrator: Bob Dinetz.

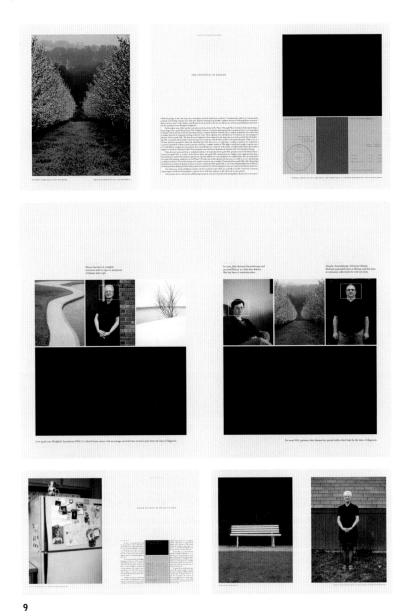

9

9. Coulter 1999 Annual Report. Creative director:
Bill Cahan. Art directors: Bill Cahan,
Sharrie Brooks. Designer: Sharrie Brooks.
Photographers: Graham MacIndoe, various.

10

10. Dole Packaging. Creative director: Bill Cahan.
Art directors: Bill Cahan, Bob Dinetz.
Designer: Bob Dinetz. Illustrator: Bob Dinetz.

11

11. Consolidated Paper Promo. Creative director: Bill Cahan. Art directors: Bill Cahan, Kevin Roberson, Bob Dinetz. Designers: Bob Dinetz, Mark Giglio, Kevin Roberson. Photographers: Bob Dinetz, Mark Giglio, Graham MacIndoe, Robert Schlatter, Ken Probst, Lars Tunbjork, various. Illustrators: Bob Dinetz, Mark Giglio, Kevin Roberson. Copywriters: Bob Dinetz, Mark Giglio, Kevin Roberson.

Selbert Perkins Design
1916 Main Street
Santa Monica, California 90405
310.664.9100
www.selbertperkins.com

SELBERT PERKINS DESIGN COLLABORATIVE

Selbert Perkins Design Collaborative (SPD) is a **multi-disciplinary design firm** offering a broad range of services including brand identity design, environmental design, print and electronic communications, as well as landscape architecture, public art, and sculpture. SPD combines a **strategic, market-driven process** with strong creative resources to develop powerful, position-based communications programs that achieve measurable success for their clients. With offices in California and Massachusetts, SPD collaborates on a daily basis with architects, developers, municipalities and corporations – nationally and internationally.

Selbert Perkins Design has a strong presence in the local Los Angeles community. The firm's work can be seen virtually everywhere; at the University of Southern California, along the Santa Monica Boulevard, at Universal Studios, while arriving and departing from Union Station, and at Los Angeles International Airport where SPD designed the dramatic landmark gateway that greets millions of visitors each year. Selbert Perkins is also heavily involved internationally with numerous projects in Japan, China, Taiwan and Singapore.

The mission of Selbert Perkins Design is to create design that will **inform, educate, and entertain people around the world through the power of art, communications and environments.**

1

2

3

1. Los Angeles International Airport Gateway. Los Angeles, CA

2. The Promenade at Howard Hughes Center identity and environmental communications system. Los Angeles, CA

3. Highmark Funds print communications system. Los Angeles, CA

THE ARBORS
OF THOUSAND OAKS

1

2

1. The Arbors identity and environmental communications. Thousand Oaks, CA

2. State Street annual report and print collateral. Boston, MA

3. American West Arena environmental wayfinding system. Phoenix, AZ

3

1

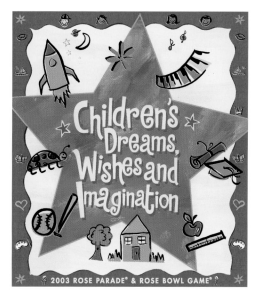

1. Tournament of Roses 2003 game and
parade collateral system. Pasadena, CA

2. Museum Square identity and
environmental communications system.
Los Angeles, CA

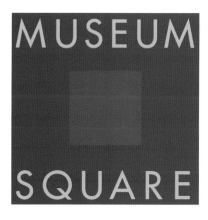

2

university park
square

1. MIT University Park environmental wayfinding system. Cambridge, MA
3. St. Bernadine Medical Center, womens' health center system. San Bernadino, CA
3. Universal Studios offices interior and exterior wayfinding. Universal Cities, CA

1

2

3

1

BINGHAM DANA

1. Bingham Dana website and print collateral system. Boston, MA

2. Union Station entrance gateways and interior/exterior wayfinding. Los Angeles, CA

2

1

SUMMER

FALL

WINTER

SPRING

1. Chia Tai Riverfest, identity and wayfinding system. Shanghai, China

2. Wan Li environmental communications, sculpture and wayfinding system. Shanghai, China

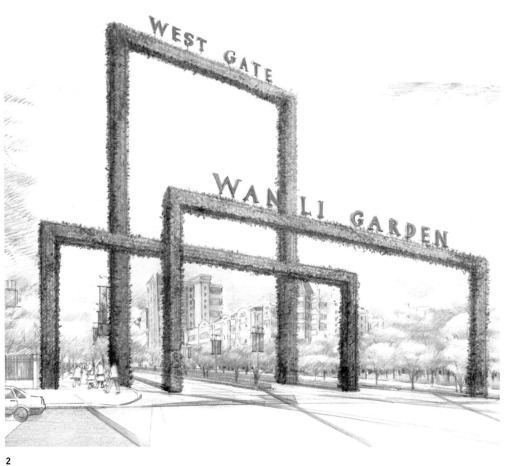

2

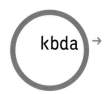 kbda →

KBDA
2558 Overland Avenue
Los Angeles, California 90064
310.287.2400
www.kbda.com

KBDA

What makes sense?

What works? What works better?

Are you feeling brave?

What are you afraid of?

Where is your future?

Are your eyes open?
Why not close them now and then?

Are you breathing?

What's the best that could happen?

Are we there yet?

Who cares?

We do.

Quite a bit, actually. Which is
why we've been asking questions of
ourselves (and our clients) for twenty
years now. We've even answered a few,
which has led to some great strategic
design for clients like Nike, UCLA, The
Getty Center, 3Com, and Hilton Hotels.

What's next?

1

2

1. Investor website for Nike, Inc.
2. Multimedia for Nike, Inc.
3. Annual report for Equity Marketing, Inc.
   (promotions and toys)

3

1

2

NEON TONIC

3

1. Annual report for
   The Macerich Company (REIT)
2. Capital campaign identity for the
   University of California at Riverside
3. Logo for on-line jazz portal

1. Capability brochure for DMX Music
2. Annual report for Micro Therapeutics, Inc. (medical devices)

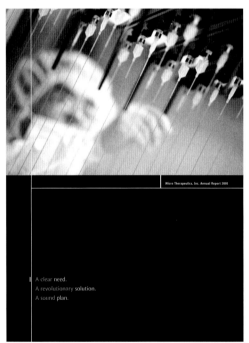

2

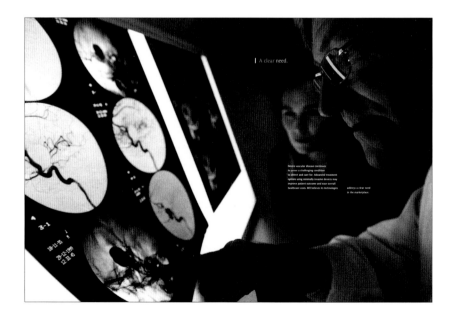

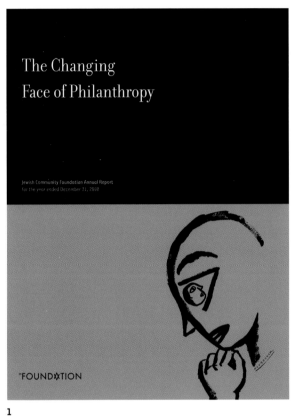

1

2

1. Annual report for The Jewish
   Community Foundation
2. Packaging for Paula's (gourmet foods)

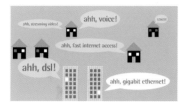

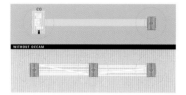

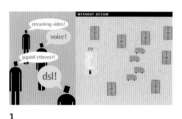

1

1. Multimedia for Occam Networks
(telecommunications)
2. Direct mail for Genex (internet development)
3. Brochure for The UCLA Foundation

2

3

1

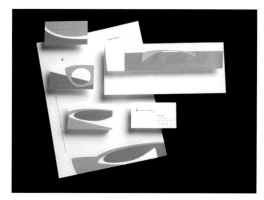

2

1. Annual report for E.piphany, Inc. (enterprise software)

2. Identity for Scaturro Sound (film and television music)

1

2

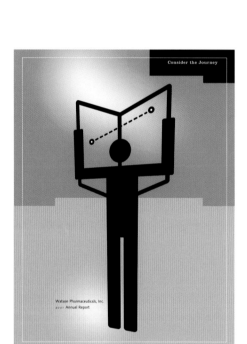

3

1. Identity for Radical Communication
(on-line advertising)

2. Website for Monterey Pop music conference

3. Annual report for Watson Pharmaceuticals, Inc.

30699 Russell Ranch Rd.

Westlake Village, California 91362

Toll Free: 877.854.8700

Main: 818.716.2613

Fax: 818.716.2661

info@dupuisgroup.com

www.dupuisgroup.com

DUPUIS

Creating Client to Customer Connections.

That's the bottom line of strategic design: forging a successful link between your brand and your buyers. That's what we've been doing since 1987: connecting our clients to their customers through standout packaging and visual identities. We've created identities, packaging and personalities for brands and products ranging from food and confection to toys, biomedical and more.

Customer connection is the commencement of our process – and its culmination. We've taken the common design process and turned it inside out to arrive at the secret of successful marketing: understanding not just how customers behave but why they behave that way.

We believe a brand is more than a well-designed logo. Brands have personality and approachability.

Customers connect to brands as they do to their friends – through common interests, values and lifestyle. They seek out those that are fun to be with, that make them feel good about themselves.

From a first-hand examination of how your buyers experience your brand in the marketplace, we create an identity that successfully speaks to them, even in a crowded retail environment.

We've built our reputation on this ability to understand customers and to integrate marketing with strategic design and breakthrough creative. Our unique work paradigm allows us to craft creative visual communications and branding and identity programs that successfully position, identify and build brand awareness and long-term customer relationships.

1.

2.

3.

4.

5

1. Foster Farms – Coastal Range Organics
   branding concept
2. Baskin Robbins – Favorite Blend branding
3. Dole – FruiTangos branding and packaging
4. Keebler – Zesta branding and
   packaging
5. Langers – Smoothie branding and packaging
6. Keebler – Sesame Street Snacks branding
   and packaging
7. Dole – Island Spice branding and packaging
   concepts

6.

7.

Above & Beyond™

1.

4.

2.

3.

1. Vankind Foods – Above & Beyond branding
2. Vankind Foods – Above & Beyond packaging
3. Baskin Robbins – Favorite Blend packaging
4. Balance Bar – Balance Bar Gold packaging concepts

1.

2.

1. Diamondback – product badge

2. Bwaries – Emporium branding

3. Encore Software – Advantage 2002 packaging

4. Munchkin – em-bry-on-ics branding
and packaging

3.

4.

1.

2.

3.

4.

1. Jamba Juice – Jamba GoGo branding
2. Jamba Juice – Jamba GoGo branding and visual identity
3. Acco Brands – Swingline architecture, structure, and packaging
4. WildSage – branding
5. Munchkin – Musical Soup branding and packaging

5.

1.

2.

3.

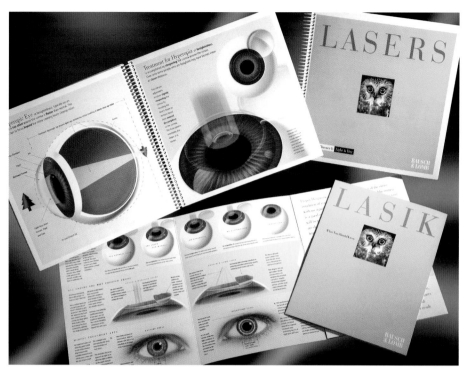

4.

5.

1. G.A.C. – corporate branding
2. Stonebridge – corporate branding
3. Intralase – corporate branding
4. Bausch & Lomb – Technolas branded collateral
5. Bausch & Lomb – Zyoptic branded collateral

1.

1. Hewlett Packard – collateral systems
2. Inova – corporate branding
3. Intellisys Group – corporate branding
4. G.A.C. – corporate collateral
5. Kodak – product collateral

2.

3.

4.

5.

1.

2.

3.

5.

Topz Restaurant

1. Interior wall graphic

2. Interior wall graphic

3. Exterior design

4. Interior design

Hana Grill

5. Stone Oven branding

4.

S T U D I O   2 0 5 5

Studio 2055
2055 Westwood Drive
Carlsbad, California 92008
760.729.8205
www.studio2055.com

Dynamic, intelligent and creative. A clear, consistent understanding of the client's expectations and goals. Exemplary service and innovative design. These virtues are responsible for the success enjoyed by Studio 2055, a smart design studio founded 20 years ago in Southern California. The premise: that fresh ideas and consistently visionary graphic solutions can succeed in an increasingly chaotic design world. It's not about the process, it's the results that matter.

The two principals, Nanette Newbry, Creative Director and fine artist; and Richard Dowdy, writer and professional photographer; head a talented team who have dedicated themselves to fulfilling the Studio's promise: Smart Thinking, Creative Solutions. Studio 2055 has

succeeded in putting its philosophy of thorough client research and intelligent resolution into every project it initiates. The inventive and effective graphic results are a testament to the ability of the creative individuals who have made the Studio's reputation for original thought and powerful communication a reality.

Their success has been built upon a foundation of creative design and smart marketing strategy in the areas of corporate identity, print collateral, Web site design, packaging and environmental graphics.

Located near the Pacific Ocean in the Village of Carlsbad, Studio 2055 stands as a beacon of intelligent design, where creativity is right at home.

1

2

3

4

1. American Cancer Society:
   Identity and Collateral for
   golf tournament sponsored
   by Harley Davidson

2. Puma: Brand Identity
   for soccer shoes for
   young women

3. Toyota Grand Prix of
   Long Beach: Poster
   featuring original
   photography by Richard Dowdy

4. Phoenix Grand Prix Association:
   Poster featuring original
   photography by Richard Dowdy

1. Montecito Partners: Identity for new home development
2. Urban Growers: Brand Identity for a foundation that restores city parks
3. SOS Printing: *Paradise Revisited*, original painting by Nanette Newbry, for the PIA Show San Diego. *Taste of Paradise*, Promotional Calendar featuring vintage pineapple advertising
4. Taylor Made/adidas Golf: Environmental Fleet Graphics

1. Photron USA:
   Corporate and Product
   Identity, Collateral,
   Web site for high-speed
   video cameras

2. Westwood Publishers
   Group: *Snap Judgments*
   book featuring original
   writing by Richard
   Dowdy

3. Twentieth Century Fox:
   X-Files: The Game,
   original concept and
   screenplay

1

2

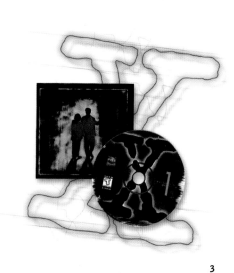

3

X-Files: The Game
Richard Dowdy created the concept and
massive 700-page script for this seven-
CD interactive, live-action game that has
sold over a million copies worldwide.

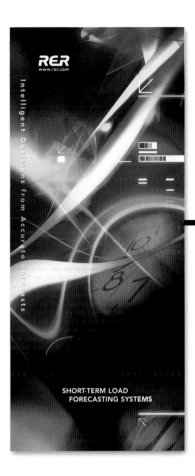

1

1. Regional Economic Research:
Product Branding, Brochures
and Packaging for energy
forecasting software

2. Directed Electronics: Product
Branding and Packaging for
high-end audio equipment

2

1. California Center for the Arts, Escondido: *Blast Off!* and *To the Moon and Beyond* joint exhibitions. Event Identity, Collateral and Environmental Design

2. University of San Diego: Brochure distributed to visitors and new students

3. Stolichnaya Gold Vodka: Special Edition Packaging

1

2

3

1. Studio 2055: Self-Promotion Calendar, *Off the Beaten Path*, featuring original photography by Richard Dowdy

2. San Diego Performing Arts League: *Bravo San Diego*. Event Identity, Collateral, Event Graphics

the mural project

may 5 2000

la fuerze de las mujeres

latina center

1

ARTISAN HERBS

2

3

4

HeartWave

helping women achieve vocational employment

5

cahuilla mountain farms

6

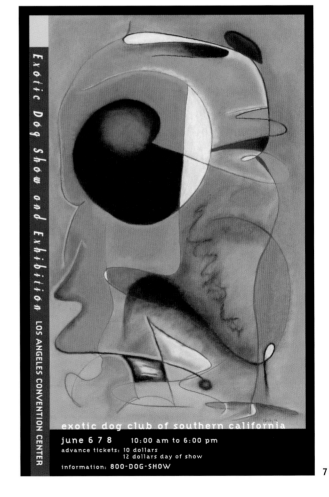

Exotic Dog Show and Exhibition LOS ANGELES CONVENTION CENTER

exotic dog club of southern california

june 6 7 8   10:00 am to 6:00 pm
advance tickets: 10 dollars
12 dollars day of show
information: 800-DOG-SHOW

7

1. Mental Health Systems: Poster and Mural for the Latina Center, CalWorks, State of California

2. Artisan Herbs: Brand Identity for herb grower

3. Ric Moore Designs: Identity for designer who makes radical golf clubs

4. Cahuilla Mountain Farms: Brand Identity for hot sauce label

5. HeartWave: Identity for a support program helping women get back to work from welfare

6. Cahuilla Mountain Farms: Organic farm producer located in the Cahuilla Valley

7. Exotic Dog Club of Southern California: *BOW-WOW*, original drawing by Nanette Newbry, for show and exhibition Poster

Nexus Design+Marketing Inc.
1510 Gershwin Street
Cardiff by the Sea, California 92007
760.635.3636

www.nexusdesigninc.com

NEXUS DESIGN+MARKETING INC.

He was a young man of 16 who loved to draw cars – big cars, fast cars, all types of cars. Who knew back then that his passion for drawing would turn into a lifelong career? Craig Calsbeek searched for a school that would let him draw all day long and began a four-year stint at Art Center College of Design in Los Angeles.

After college Craig became a professional freelance illustrator with representation on both coasts. He served as Creative Director for a large local publisher and worked in a freelance capacity with many national advertising agencies.

Nexus Design + Marketing, Inc. was formed over 20 years ago in Santa Monica, Calif., and the firm has been creating award-winning work ever since. A communications firm, Nexus specializes in promotions, direct mail, press relations campaigns, magazine editorial, POP materials, direct response campaigns, annual reports, printed ads, collateral materials of all sizes and shapes, billboards, banners and websites.

Nexus has worked with a diverse array of companies, from international corporations to fiercely independent start-ups. The firm has completed countless annual reports, collateral, digital media, identity, and packaging assignments.

The methodology is simple: Craig believes that successful ideas are generated from creative partnerships. Nexus involves its clients from the beginning in the creative process and they work together closely throughout the entire project.

Through the years Nexus has been known as the "small design firm on steroids" and has remained a small company by choice. At Nexus, clients work directly with the principals – seasoned professionals who understand evolving marketing challenges and continue to refine their craft. By keeping the overhead low, Nexus is the first choice of many smart companies nationwide.

The firm continues to effectively deliver better results, faster and more efficiently.

1

2

3

5

6

4

1. Colortek, corporate identity
2. City of Santa Monica. Bayside District logo
3. Los Angeles Culinary Institute logo
4. McIntosh Labs, corporate identity
5. Dep Corporation, Agree Shampoo packaging
6. Bayside District logo signage applications
7. McIntosh Labs, full line product ad campaign

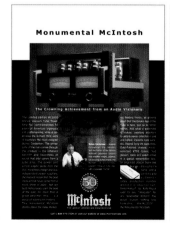

7

1. Baseline Consulting stationary package
2. Baseline Consulting corporate identity
3. Chant Voice Recognition software logo
4. KB Homes logo proposal
5. Clarion Car Audio product catalog
6. Clarion Car Audio Multimedia poster

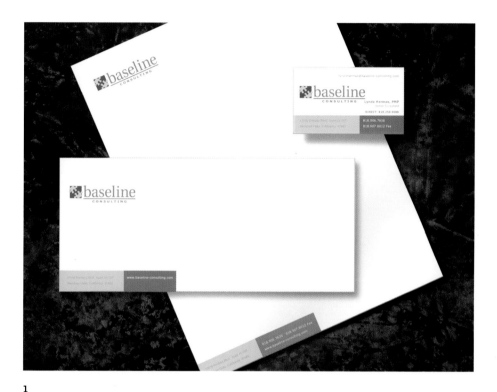

1

2

3

4

5

6

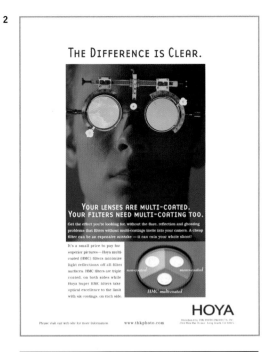

1. Clarion Surround Sight full page ad
2. Hoya Filters full page ad
3. Herbie Hancock at the Hollywood Bowl poster
4. Kenwood Video Toolkit package
5. Kenwood Portable Headphone packages

1. Kenko Lens website
2. Hotel Oceana website
3. Yo Racers product logo
4. City of Glendale Exchange Shopping Center logo
5. Get Liste Web Listing Service logo
6. Bill Ratner Voice-Over Audio Demo package
7. Karma Police logo
8. Kenwood Sales Kit brochure
9. Kenwood Marine Audio product catalog

3

1

2

4

5

4

6

7

8

9

1

2

Hard Rock Hotel

1. Classic logo
2. Corporate identity
3. Product logo applications
4. NFR Rodeo "Rock'n Horses" event logo
5. Facility logo
6. Holiday card
7. Coin collectible package
8. Newsletter
9. Salsa package
10. Casino chips

3

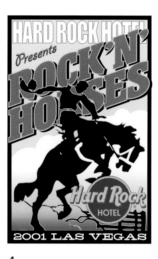

4

5

6

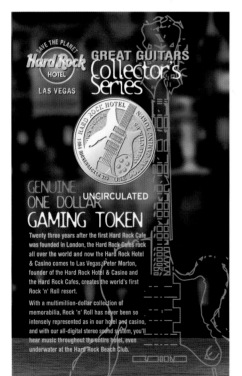

7

8

9

10

1

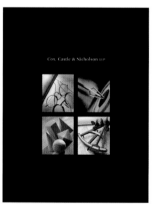

2

3

4

5

6

7

239

1

2

3

4

5

6

7

1. GottaGettaGift Holiday gift basket catalog
2. Clarion Car Audio AutoPC® logo
3. Velodyne Acoustics velomotive logo
4. Bravo Cucina Italian Restaurant logo
5. Paracel Sequence Analysis ad
6. Epson printer hang tag promotion package
7. Slik Tripods product catalog
8. A-1 Metal website
9. Hotel Oceana website

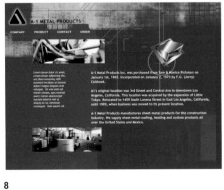

8

9

2045 Kettner Blvd, Ste 101
San Diego, CA 92101
P 619.238.4555
F 619.238.0555
bennett@pejidesign.com
www.pejidesign.com

BENNETT PEJI DESIGN

Left to Right: Clarissa Vendemiatti, Rick Dominguez, Lilia Peji (seated), Bennett Peji, Stefan Hontschik, Nick Inzunza

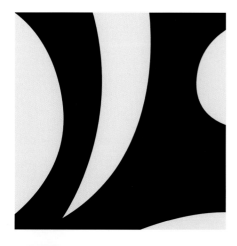

In order to produce the most effective graphic design solutions, we do our background research and develop as complete a knowledge as is possible about our clients and their position. We review the company's mission statement and position in the marketplace, its history, customers and investors, as well as how they are perceived by employees, customers and outsiders. We get to understand the company's philosophy,

culture and specific goals. We also review their competitors' positions and marketing materials for their strengths and weaknesses as well as all the clients own existing materials for coherency - or lack of it. With this information, together, we define the design parameters. This consists of a written branding statement and a list of 4 or 5 objectives that the design solution must accomplish. By thoroughly defining the criteria, a truly

unique and appropriate solution will be achieved. Because we've learned each project's unique characteristics, needs and audience, we avoid designing from preconceived ideas. And doing this homework up front actually streamlines the creative process. We don't waste time pursuing inappropriate directions. In fact, if the analysis is done succinctly enough, sometimes the perfect solution emerges itself.

INF CUS

ountain Valley, 1989   Mark Klett (b. 19.   lbany, New York)
Gelatin silver prir
Lent by the artist

MUSEUM   PHOTOGRAPHIC ARTS

NEWSLETTER

Finding and revealing the essence of the client's position in the marketplace is always the challenge of the design process. It can only be accomplished consistently by doing a lot of research on the client and their industry, asking the right questions, and listening with an open mind. We then take the client's mission statement and develop a branding statement. A mission statement says what the organization does, however, a

branding statement says how the organization does it in their unique, memorable way. A branding statement focuses on the PR value of the organization and its deeper connection with its constituents. Our job is to find an authentic, core message that will remain true for the organization for as long as it exists. The challenge for MoPA was to portray a timeless quality, since the museum's collection and exhibits cover the entire 150

year history of photography including the most current trends, plus communicate the concept of photography and do so in a way that suggests the growing stature of MoPA as one of the premier photography institutions in the country. No matter how much the technology and equipment change, the essence of photography will always be about capturing light. And that's what we've done with the distinctive background. Also, having

the light and shadow design come from off the page from all four sides symbolizes the photographic aspects of "capturing the moment" both in time and space. The design captures a portion of an environment that goes well beyond its borders. The MoPA logo itself portrays the "museum" and "art" parts of the name. It represents art within a structure... a building that exhibits the photographic works of art, as distinguished from a

photographer or photo lab. The stationery design radiates a rich and ethereal monochromatic color scheme. Similar to a classic, toned photo print. Whether designed 10 years ago, yesterday, or 10 years from now, the design will always be an appropriate and distinctive asset for the client.

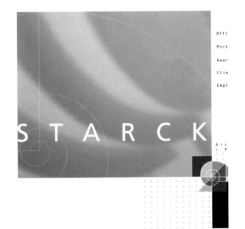

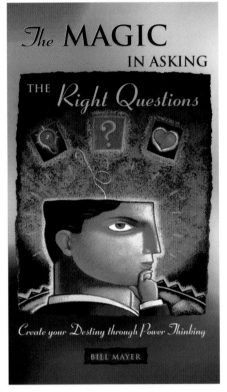

▶ Starck Architecture and Planning web site
www.starckap.com

◀ Logo for the Hewlett-Packard
line of Color Copiers

▶ The Magic in Asking the Right
Questions, book design

◀ Packaging for ONTRO, the first self-heating
beverage container in the U.S. market

▶ City Moves, after school
arts program identity

The mission of City Moves is to empower
children, through dance, to create, build
relationships, and connect to community.

▼ Industrial graphics for HP Fax Machine

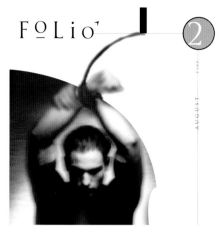

FOLIo 2

PRIME 10 STEAKHOUSE

2

▶ Cover design for Folio Magazine

⬥ Restaurant identity for
Prime 10 Steakhouse

▼ Industrial graphics for Hewlett-Packard

▶ E TIX Today logo

The Etix logo for the San Diego
Performing Arts League entices you to
buy your tickets online by reminding
you of the drama and excitement of an
opening night with a searchlight and an
active, jumping ticket

⬥ Ziro clock catalog

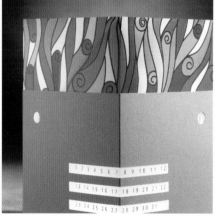

⬥ Packaging for Bread & Cie Bakery

◀ Dimensional design for luminary
calendar with interchangeable inserts

▼ Logo for Baja California
Missions Foundation

◐ The Scripps Institute web site
www.scripps.edu

◓ Corporate identity for AUGEN, Mexico's
largest optical manufacturer

◒ County of San Diego District Attorney web
site www.sandiegoda.com

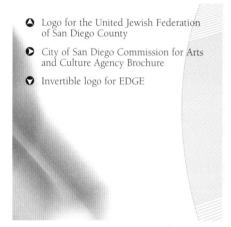

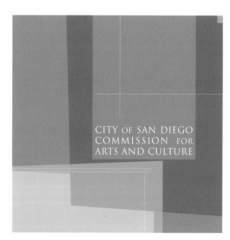

◓ Logo for the United Jewish Federation
of San Diego County

◐ City of San Diego Commission for Arts
and Culture Agency Brochure

◒ Invertible logo for EDGE

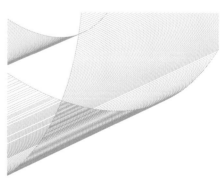

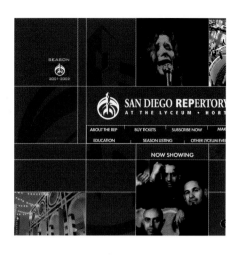

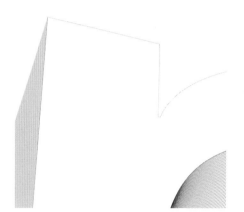

- San Diego Repertory Theatre web site
  www.sandiegorep.com
- FinaBaby premium products brand
- Inventing the Child, book design
- Hewlett-Packard package design
- San Diego Printing Industry Association
  poster design

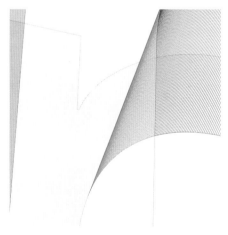

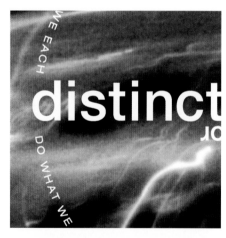

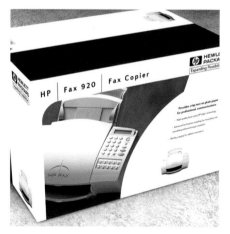

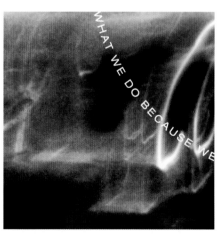

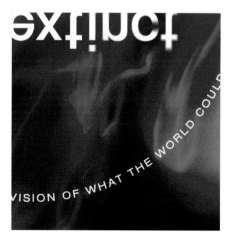

ex

◀ "Design Garden" environmental design

Our mission is to help our clients become distinct, not extinct, through smart branding. Our job is to make visible the company's strategy and project an enhanced commitment to a clear and comprehensible vision. Our vision is to symbolize the corporate ethos, its attitudes, so that everyone who works for the organization can share the same spirit and then communicate it to all the people who deal with the organization.

in

ct

20/02 VISION

THE THOMPSON DESIGN GROUP

The Thompson Design Group
725 Greenwich Street, Suite 300
San Francisco, California 94133
T 415.982.5827
www.ttdg.com

Since 1978 Thompson Design Group has been dedicated to achieving client goals by producing highly creative, innovative and effective design solutions. With Principals Jody Thompson and Dennis Thompson, Thompson Design is comprised of a team of focused and experienced design and marketing communicators.

Headquartered in San Francisco, Thompson Design Group specializes in designing and developing corporate, product, service and retail brands with expertise in:

- Brand Identity
- Naming and Naming Systems - *NameWorks*™
- Package Design and Visual Branding Systems
- Corporate Identity
- Branded Environments
- Brand Equity Management

Whether the project is a new identity for a brand or a company, or a packaging revitalization and restaging, the firm's strategic thinking provides uncompromising design solutions.

1

2

3

4

1. Toll House Refrigerated Cookie Dough
2. Betty Crocker Bac-Os
3. General Mills Basic 4 Cereal
4. Foster Farms Corn Dogs Line
5. Cascadian Farm Frozen Lines
6. Del Monte Savory Sensations
7. Dreyer's/Starbucks Frappuccino Bars

5

6

7

1

3

2

1. Nestea Concentrate Tea

2. Nesquik Hot Cocoa Mix

3. Nesquik RTD Line Extension

4. Nestea Soluble Iced Tea

5. Freemark Abbey Core Wines

6. Buena Vista Reserve Wines

7. Armida Wines

8. Clorox Disinfecting Sprays

9. Optimize Nutraceutical Beverages

10. Dixie SureStone Packaging Concepts

4

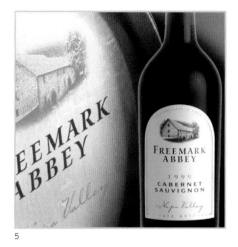

5

6

7

8

9

10

1. Nestlé Classic Scream Collection
2. Nestlé WonderBall Seasonal
3. Nestlé Crunch Shaq Promotion
4. Nestlé Treasures Seasonal
5. Spiedini Restaurant Identity
6,7. DHL Fleet Design
8. Nestea NASCAR Concepts

5

6

8

7

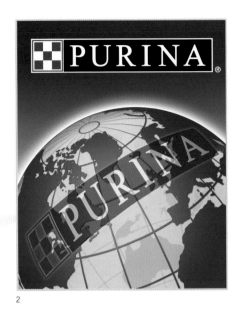

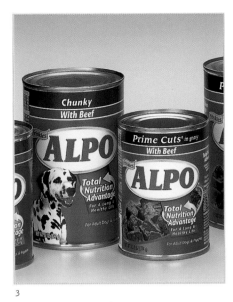

1. Friskies Cat Treats
2. Purina Identity Poster
3. Alpo Canned
4. Mighty Dog Pouch
5. Fancy Feast Canned
6. Friskies Special Needs
7. Scoop Away Clean

For effective brandesign, global brands turn to the man with one hell of a good eye.

Mike Salisbury, LLC
Effective Brandesign
P.O. box 2309
Venice, California 90294
310.392.8779
mikesalcom@attbi.com

MIKE SALISBURY LLC

To accept that a brand idea-rather than a simple logo or ad-can drive a communications program, requests a radical change in thinking for some.

We have been fortunate to be associated with a variety of very successful companies. In gaining that experience we've learned a lot about the things that make brands work and the things that don't work.

Brands are the basis for a sustainable marketing and merchandising advantage for organizations.

Branding projects which involve visual identity are more than a one-shot deal.

They are long-term graphic investments.

An advertising campaign can have a life span of several years.

Packaging is rarely changed, and then only subtly.

Corporate identity programs can continue on for decades.

To build a brand you need a good brand strategist:

-Creative in proposing communications solutions.

-Well-versed in alternative media.

-Excellent in execution, particularly in developing themes and visual imagery.

-An objective voice in client matters.

Strong brand ideas do not just happen. They result from a future-oriented,strategic visionary process lead by an innovative communication team.

We of course think that is
Mike Salisbury LLC.

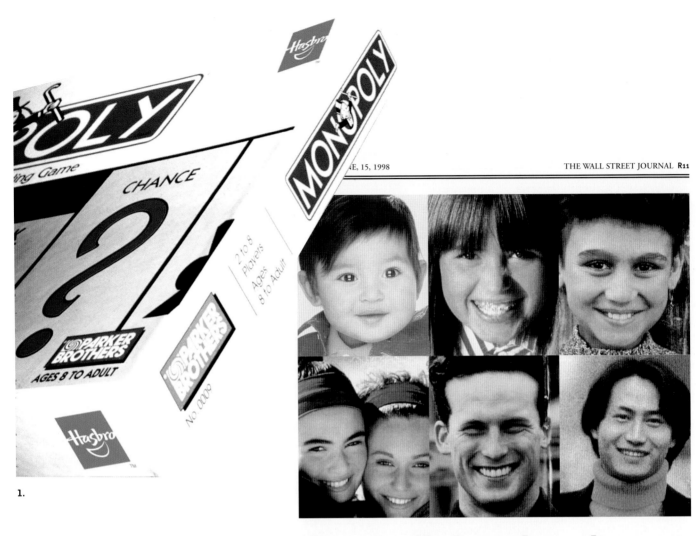

1.

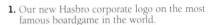

3.

We proudly introduce the most imitated logo on earth.

See? You're imitating it right now. And you're not even playing Monopoly or Star Wars or Mr. Potato Head or G.I. Joe, or with Nerf balls or Tonka Trucks.

But you have, and you will.

And every time they make you smile, if you look closely, you'll see our smile grow just a little brighter.

2.

1. Our new Hasbro corporate logo on the most famous boardgame in the world.

2. Wall Street Journal ad created by Mike Salisbury, LLC to introduce the newly created brand image that represents the family of the world's best known toys to the global financial markets as one entity.

3. Cross marketing the corporate brand and the world's favorite game brands with our designs for the Hasbro communication systems.

4. Hasbro corporate internet site featuring their new smile-the world's most well known symbol for fun and Hasbro's most important product.

[before]

™

[after]

4.

The book that tells you exactly how to create strong
brands, ads, logos, apparel, collateral, tv and publications.
Get your copy today from www.amazon.com